The Stained Glass Classroom

The Stained Glass Classroom

Projects Using Copper Foil,
Lead & Mosaic Techniques

Vicki Payne

Sterling Publishing Co., Inc.
New York

Prolific Impressions Production Staff:

Editor in Chief: Mickey Baskett
Copy Editor: Phyllis Mueller
Graphics: Lampe-Farley Communications
Styling: Lenos Key
Photography: Jerry Mucklow
Administration: Jim Baskett

Library of Congress Cataloging-in-Publication Data

Payne, Vicki.
Stained glass classroom, the: projects using copper foil, lead & mosaic techniques / Vicki Payne.
  p. cm.
  Includes index
  ISBN 1-4027-1407-6
1. Glass painting and staining. 2. Glass craft. I. Title.
  TT298.P3797 2004
  748.5--dc22

2004012130

10 9 8 7 6 5 4 3 2

Published by Sterling Publishing Co., Inc.
387 Park Avenue South, New York, N.Y. 10016

©2004 by Prolific Impressions, Inc.
Produced by Prolific Impressions, Inc.
160 South Candler St., Decatur, GA 30030

Distributed in Canada by Sterling Publishing
c/o Canadian Manda Group, 165 Dufferin St., Toronto, Ontario, Canada M6K 3H6
Distributed in Great Britain by Chrysalis Books Group PLC,
The Chrysalis Building, Bramley Road, London W10 6SP, England
Distributed in Australia by Capricorn Link (Australia) Pty. Ltd.
P.O. Box 704, Windsor, NSW 2756 Australia
Printed in China
All rights reserved
Sterling ISBN 1-4027-1407-6

For information about custom editions, special sales, premium and corporate purchases, please contact Sterling Special Sales Department at 800-805-5489 or specialsales@sterlingpub.com

Acknowledgements

The author wishes to thank the following companies for providing supplies used in this book:

American Bevel
www.americanbevel.com

Cascade Lead Products
1614 West 75th Ave.
Vancouver, BC V6P 6G2

Cooper Tools/Weller
P.O. Box 728
Apex, NC 27502
www.coppertools.com

Vic's Crafts
www.glasswithvickipayne.com

Glastar Corporation
www.glastar.com

Glass Accessories International
www.glassaccessories.com

Special thanks to Cindy Oppenheim, Vicki's studio assistant.

About Vicki Payne

Vicki Payne is an educational leader of the home decor and crafting industries. As CEO of Cutters Productions, she produces the nationally syndicated television shows: *Glass with Vicki Payne*; *Paint! Paint! Paint!*, *One Stroke Painting*, *Kid Concoctions, Savvy Senior,* and *For Your Home*, which she co-hosts with her daughter, Sloan Rutter. Together, these weekly 30-minute programs are carried by more than a 160 different public television stations and GoodLife TV on cable. In addition to hosting her own shows, Vicki is the host of *D.I.Y. Handmade Gifts* on HGTV's D.I.Y. Network. She is a frequent guest on home improvement and crafting shows, including *The Carol Duvall Show, Home Matters, Kitty Bartholomew: Your Home,* and *Decorating with Style.*

Vicki has produced how-to videos for over 15 years, created her own certified teacher program, is frequently published in craft and trade magazines, and serves as a consultant to companies throughout the craft and hobby industries. She has succeeded by sharing her passion by making her talents accessible to others.

Vicki is the author of *Stained Glass in an Afternoon* (Sterling, 2002) and *Traditional Leaded Glass Crafting* (Sterling, 2003). A member of the Art Glass Association (AGA) Board of Directors, Hobby International Association, and Association of Creative Crafts. Vicki also owns and operates *Vic's Crafts*, an internet shopping site supplying videos, kits, supplies, and education to all types of crafters, decorators, and do-it-yourselfers.

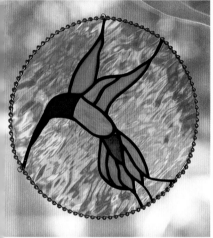

STAINED GLASS CLASSROOM

Three Methods of Stained Glass Crafting

Who hasn't admired the beauty of stained glass and marveled at the rich colors, the gorgeous textures, the sparkle of the glass, the soft gleam of metal edging? But chances are you thought stained glass wasn't something you could make—it seemed so difficult, so time-consuming. Think again!

This book will introduce you to three different techniques for crafting beautiful stained glass pieces—the lead came method, the copper foil method, and the mosaic method. For each technique, you'll learn how to choose supplies and tools. Then you'll be shown, in a step-by-step photo series, how easy it is to prepare, cut, assemble, and finish a sample project. A collection of beautiful projects for each technique follows the basic instructions.

The Lead Came Method

The lead came method is the more traditional technique of crafting stained glass. Pieces of glass are cut and fit into metal channels called cames. Came comes in a variety of sizes and metal types; the most common is lead, but you will also find came made from hard metals such as zinc, brass, and copper.

The places where cames meet or intersect within a project are called joints. The joints are soldered to create a strong, continuous metal frame around each individual glass piece within the project.

The Copper Foil Method

Most beginners start with the copper foil method. First, pieces of stained glass are cut by the pattern shapes. Then, the edges of these pieces are covered with a copper (or other metal) foil tape, and the wrapped pieces are assembled on a surface as if they were parts of a jigsaw puzzle. The metal tape around the pieces becomes a base for a bead of solder that connects all the foil-edged shapes. The copper foil method is great for panels and sconces, lampshades, and boxes.

The Glass Mosaic Method

Stained glass adds beauty and sparkle to mosaic projects. (Perhaps that's why some early mosaics were made from glass.) This method of crafting with stained glass is like making tile mosaics, but instead of opaque ceramic tile pieces, the mosaic "tile" is stained glass. Stained glass mosaics have a brilliant, luminescent quality.

This book also includes a bonus project that defies classification. It's a wind chime made with a recycled dish that's held together with wire, and it further illustrates the versatility of crafting with stained glass.

Supplies for Getting Started

Stained Glass

The terms "stained glass" and "art glass" are interchangeable—both are used to describe types of glass manufactured for decorative purposes, as opposed to "flat" or "float" glass, which is commonly used for auto glass, windows, and doors.

There are two basic categories of stained glass: opalescent and cathedral. **Opalescent glass** is glass you cannot easily see through; **cathedral glass** is glass you can see through more clearly. Within each category there are unlimited variations and combinations of colors, textures, densities, and patterns.

For the past few decades, the most popular type of "stained" glass isn't colored glass—it's clear art glass. Its endless variety of textures, patterns, and iridized finishes has captured my interest as an artist for over 25 years. Every time I see a new piece of glass, I can't wait to cut and shape it into my newest project.

Glass is sold by the square foot or by the pound. If you buy glass by the square foot, you get a piece of glass that is 12" x 12". If you buy glass by the pound, you generally get 1-1/2 pounds of glass to the square foot. It is a good rule of thumb to buy about 25 percent more glass than the size of your project; you may use more than you anticipated. It is always a heartbreaker to go back to the glass shop and discover there is no more of the glass you need in stock and to have to wait for the next shipment to come in. "Always buy more" is a good rule of thumb—you can use it for a future project if it's left over. Glass costs between $2.50 and $7 a square foot, depending on the color of the glass.

When choosing glass colors, the best rule of thumb is to buy what you like. If you like pink, use pink. If you like yellow, select yellow. Feel free to change the colors of any of the projects in this book to suit your taste or your decor.

Stained glass **rondels** are handmade glass circles that have been used for centuries to fashion door and window panels. They come in a wide variety of colors and sizes. They can be used as accents or as central motifs in panels.

Glass nuggets are flat on the back and rounded on the top. They come in a variety of shapes and colors and can be used as accents or as the main pieces for fanciful sculptural designs.

Glass Types & Textures

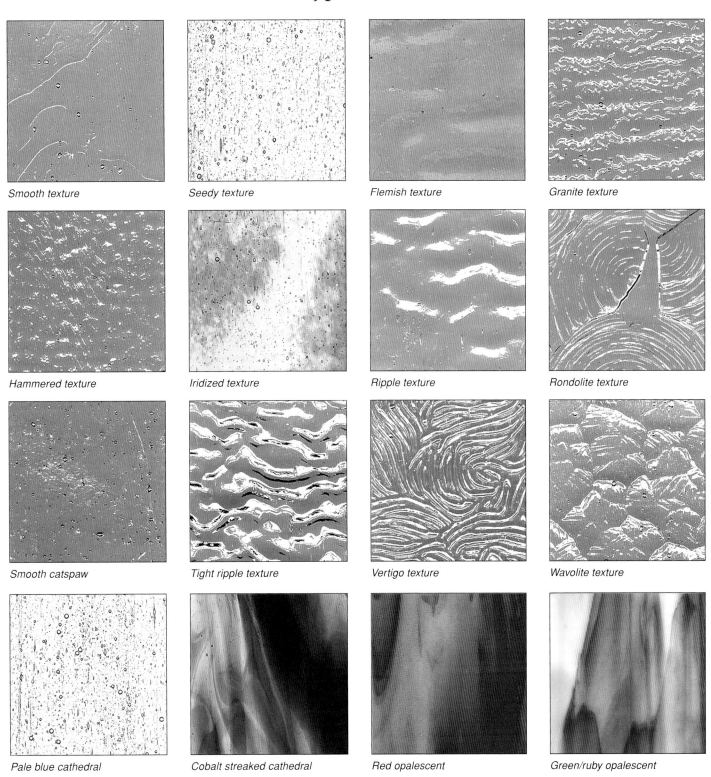

Smooth texture

Seedy texture

Flemish texture

Granite texture

Hammered texture

Iridized texture

Ripple texture

Rondolite texture

Smooth catspaw

Tight ripple texture

Vertigo texture

Wavolite texture

Pale blue cathedral

Cobalt streaked cathedral

Red opalescent

Green/ruby opalescent

Glass Cutting Tools

Glass cutters are the tools used to score glass so it can be cut. The score, a barely visible scratch or fissure made on the surface of the glass by the metal wheel of the cutter, weakens the glass at the site of the score and makes it easier to break.

Carbide Cutters

Handheld **carbide cutters** are the ones you'll use for most of your glass cutting. They come with different handles in a variety of styles and range in price from just a couple of dollars to about $30. The cutting wheels of all glass cutters need to be lubricated with oil, so a **self-oiling cutter** is convenient to use—it automatically lubricates the wheel as you score.

Strip Cutter

A **strip cutter** is a glass-cutting tool that can be set to a desired width. It will cut straight, parallel, uniform strips of glass again and again. It's especially useful for making boxes.

Strip-Circle Cutter

A **strip-circle cutter** is a glass cutting tool that can be set to cut both strips and circles in a range of sizes.

Lubricating Oil

Lubricating oil is necessary to protect the cutting wheel so the glass cutter will last much longer and because a score line which has been lubricated with oil is much easier to break.

If your cutter is not self-oiling, you'll need to saturate a towel with lubricating oil and keep it handy. Pass the wheel of the cutter over the oil-saturated towel before each score.

You can buy lubricating oil or mix your own. I like to use a mixture of equal amounts of motor oil and lamp oil.

Glass Saw

For cutting thicker, wavy glass, such as drapery glass, A glass saw is recommended.

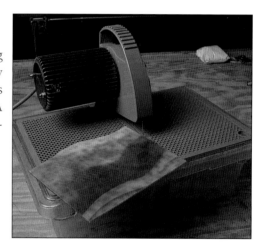

Safety Gear

Protective Glasses

Always wear **protective glasses, goggles, or a face shield** when cutting and grinding glass to shield your eyes from glass chips and fragments and splattering flux or solder.

Face Mask

When you are soldering, wear a **face mask** specially designed to protect you from soldering fumes. They are available at stained glass stores and hardware stores. **Always** work in a well-ventilated area when soldering.

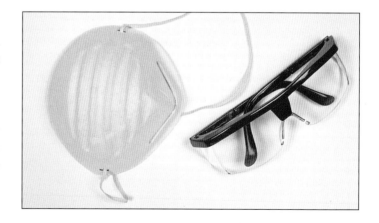

Pictured opposite, top to bottom, on left: brass-handled cutter, comfort grip cutter, Thompson grip cutter, pistol grip cutter. At right: a strip cutter.

CAUTION!

Certain precautions should be taken when working with lead came, glass, and chemicals.

- The glass studio is not a place for small children, and older children should always be supervised when they are working with stained glass tools and materials.
- Lead came is toxic when mishandled. Keep your hands away from your mouth while working in lead. Make sure to wash your hands with warm water and soap before leaving your studio. If you feel like a snack, take a break. Don't eat or drink in your studio.
- Always work in a well-lighted, well-ventilated area.

Glass Breaking Tools

Glass breaking tools can be used as extensions of your hands to hold and break glass.

Running Pliers

Running pliers have curved jaws with a raised ridge on the bottom and a location the ridge fits into on the top. Use running pliers to help you push the score line through the glass so you can break it with the pliers instead of with your hands. The mark on the top jaw helps you position the pliers on the score line.

Breaking Pliers

Breaking pliers have jaws that are flat on the inside. When you need to hold a piece of glass to break it and do not have room for two hands, use these.

Grozing Pliers

Grozing pliers have little teeth like a file on both the top and the bottom jaws. Use these pliers to chip away at the little unwanted pieces of glass that remain along a cut after scoring and breaking.

Combination Pliers

Combination pliers have a flat jaw and a curved jaw. Both jaws are serrated. Combination pliers can be used both for breaking and grozing. Use the curved side up for grozing and the flat side up for breaking.

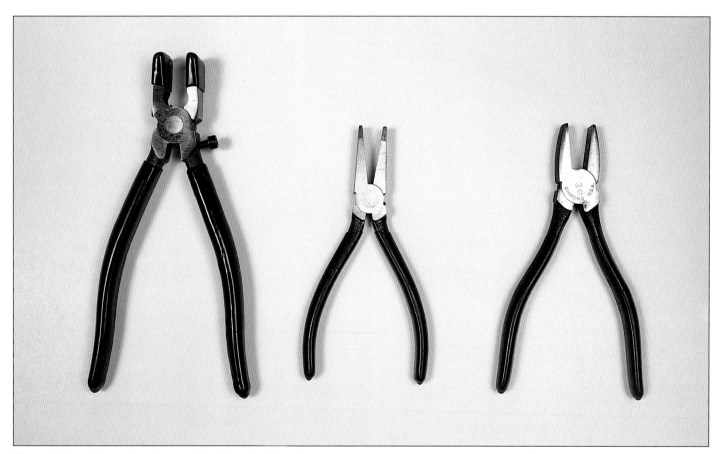

Pictured left to right: running pliers, grozing pliers, breaking pliers.

Glass Smoothing Supplies

Glass smoothing supplies prepare the edges of cut glass pieces for the application of copper foil and correct minor problems in the shape of a piece of glass, ensuring that pieces will fit together as intended.

Glass Grinder

An electric **glass grinder** is a machine with a diamond bit and a tray underneath the bit that contains water. There is a sponge in the back that pumps water up to the bit to keep it wet when you are grinding. The water keeps the dust down and keeps the glass cool so it will not fracture.

A grinder is the fastest, most efficient way to prepare glass pieces and correct problems on the edges of pieces, but grinders are not inexpensive. You might want to check with your local glass shop about renting one. When you use a glass grinder, **always** wear safety glasses and follow the manufacturer's instructions.

Emery Cloth/Carborundum Stone

An **emery cloth** or a **carborundum stone** also may be used to smooth the edges of cut glass pieces. Be forewarned that using a carborundum stone or emery cloth is a slow process, but it's less expensive than buying a grinder.

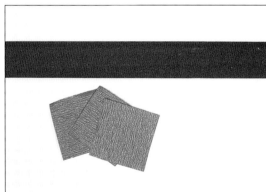

Pictured top to bottom: Carborundum stone, emery cloth.

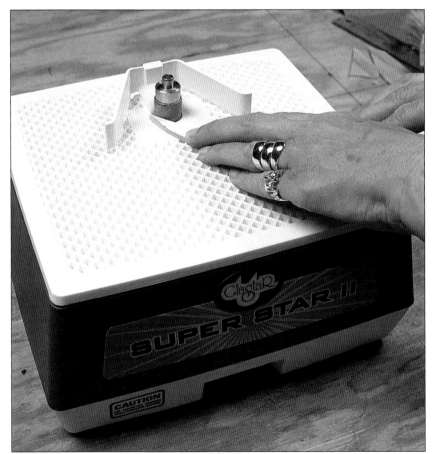

A glass grinder.

Pattern Making Supplies

When you are first starting out, it is better to use a pattern designed specifically for stained glass. When you become more experienced, you can create your own designs. Use these supplies to make patterns for cutting out glass pieces and assembling your projects.

Pattern Paper

I like to use **white bond paper or white craft paper** for patterns—white instead of brown because it is easier to see the colors of colored pencils. If you use a light box for tracing the pattern lines on the glass, white paper is easier to see through.

Tracing Paper

Use **tracing paper** and a **pencil** to trace patterns from this (and other) books. Buy tracing paper at crafts and art supply stores.

Transfer Paper

Use **transfer paper** to transfer designs to pattern paper. You also can use a photocopier to make copies of traced designs.

Colored Pencils

Cutting the pieces for your stained glass projects is easier if you take the time to color in the design with **colored pencils**. That way, you create a color-keyed pattern that's especially helpful when you cut apart the pattern to make templates for cutting.

Ruler

The most important tool you need is a **metal ruler**. An 18" ruler is a good size to have. Make sure it's calibrated from one end all the way to the other. Also make sure it has a cork back. This will prevent it from slipping around while you are drawing and using it as you cut glass.

Pattern Shears

Stained glass is composed of pieces of glass separated by pieces of metal all the way across a project, and the metal takes up space between each piece of glass. When you cut out pattern pieces with **pattern shears** to make templates for cutting your glass, the special blades of the pattern shears (there are three of them) remove a small strip of paper on the cutting lines to allow space for the metal.

You might want to practice cutting with pattern shears on some scrap paper before you cut out your pattern to make templates.

Rubber Cement

Use **rubber cement** or a **pattern fixative** to hold pattern pieces in place for cutting and grinding. Either will simply rub off the glass when you're ready to construct your piece.

Masking Tape

You also need **masking tape** to hold your design in place on your work board and for holding pieces of glass for birdhouses, lampshades, and boxes together until you solder them.

Markers

To mark on glass, choose markers that aren't permanent on glass and can be rubbed or washed off. Test **felt-tip markers** on a scrap of glass before using. A **china marker**, available at crafts and art supply stores in a variety of colors, is another good choice for marking glass.

Other Supplies

It is a good idea to get a **shoebox** to put your cut-apart pattern pieces in so you don't lose any of them. If you do happen to lose a pattern piece during the process of building your window, you can always make a tracing off your other (un-cut) copy.

Soldering Tools & Supplies

Soldering is done on both the copper foil and lead came methods.
For soldering, you need the following supplies:

Flux and Brush

Flux is a cleaner that prepares metal to accept the solder. Without flux, soldering isn't possible. I recommend a water-soluble flux, which can be washed off your project with dishwashing soap and water and can be left on your project overnight or until the next day without doing damage.

When you're working, it's a good idea to pour some flux out of the container it comes in and into a wide-mouth jar. Don't ever go back and forth from the container the flux comes in to your project. You'll weaken the strength of the flux if you do.

Apply flux to your project with a **flux brush**. These brushes rust out after a while (continuing exposure to the flux corrodes them), so it's a good idea to buy a couple at a time.

Solder

Solder is the molten metal used to join the metal-wrapped glass pieces in the copper foil technique and secure the joints in metal came. Solder looks like thick wire and comes on a spool. When doing the leaded glass technique, you'll work with a solid-core solder labeled "50/50." The numbers indicate what percentage tin (50%) and lead (50%) are in the solder.

Soldering Iron with Rheostat

To solder stained glass, you need a **soldering iron**, not a soldering gun. You can't use a soldering gun on a stained glass project. The **rheostat** controls the temperature of the soldering iron. Soldering irons come with tips of various sizes. For many copper foil projects, a tip 1/4" wide is used.

An **iron stand** keeps your iron from rolling around on your work surface and protects you from the hot parts of the iron when you are working.

Tip Cleaner

A **tip cleaner** is simply a sponge that is kept wet so that you can wipe off the tip of your soldering iron as you work to keep it clean and completely shiny. If you work with a soldering iron tip that is all dark, you won't be able to do a good job of soldering.

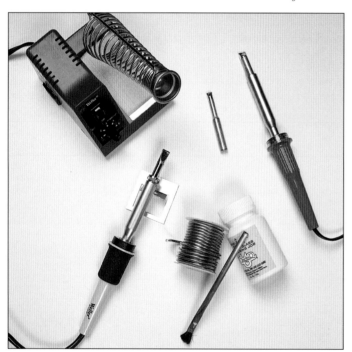

Pictured from top left: Soldering iron rheostat with iron holder, 80 watt soldering iron, flux and flux brush, solder, 100 watt thermostatically controlled soldering iron with extra tip.

Assembly Supplies

Squaring Bars

These bars are used along the outer perimeter of a panel to help you square up your project after it is built (provided, of course, that the project is square). You can make your own squaring bars by cutting various lengths of clear glass into 1-1/2" wide strips. You will need bars from 12" to 24" in length. Wrap the edges in masking tape. You can also purchase metal squaring bars.

Work Space

It is important to select a work table that is at a comfortable height with enough space to accommodate your project when it is completely built plus all the tools and supplies you need to build the project. In your work space, you also want to make sure you have good lighting, convenient access to electrical outlets, good ventilation, and a hard-surface floor that is easy to clean.

Work Boards

Your work board is the surface you'll use for assembling your glass projects. It should fit comfortably on your work table and be at least 2" bigger than the project you're making. A **plywood work board** is best for leading up panels. I like to use 3/8" or 1/2" thick plywood.

You'll need to form a right angle on two sides of your work board for leading up panels. I like to use 1" x 1" stop molding for this. Use a **carpenter's triangle** or framing square and double check the angle you construct (more than once!) to make sure it's perfectly square. If you don't start out square, you will never be able to build a square project!

For copper foil work, an option is to make a work board from **Homasote**, a building material that's often used to make bulletin boards. Buy plywood and Homasote at building supply stores.

If your work space is limited, you can make a portable work board and store it behind a door or in the garage. Don't paint or varnish your work boards; the heat of the soldering process will cause the lead came to stick to the finish.

Push pins are handy to have for help with assembly.

Tips for Successful Stained Glass

Scoring the Glass

You should score a piece of glass only once. Do not go over a score line twice—that's a good way to ruin your cutter, and your cut is not going to be successful.

Determining a Cutting Order

It's a good idea to cut the big pieces first and then the little ones. If you make a mistake you can use your scrap glass to cut out the other piece(s).

Tack-Soldering

Many times you will be instructed to "tack-solder" a project. Tack-soldering holds pieces together so they won't move as you create your solder seams.

To tack-solder, dab a small amount of flux at any point along a foil seam. Touch the solder and the hot iron to the flux for a very short time—about a second—to create a dab of molten solder. When the solder cools, it will hold the pieces of glass in place.

Soldering

- Your solder seam should be as tall as it is wide. You don't want it to be flat. You want it to have a crowned, rounded edge.
- A nice thing about copper foil soldering is that if you're not happy with the way it looks, you can re-flux and go back over it again.

- Always keep a hot liquid puddle right under your soldering tip. Let the solder flow at its own speed along with you.
- If your solder looks lumpy, you either need more flux or more heat.
- Solder from top to bottom. I like to start at the top of my window (the part that's farthest away from me) so I don't drag my sleeves through the hot solder as I go along.

Working with the Grain of the Glass

Like fabric, art glass has a grain to it. The grain runs vertically from top to bottom on a sheet of glass. In some glass types, the striations are more visible than others. It is important to take the time to determine the grain of your glass and mark the direction of the grain by drawing arrows on your glass. The arrows will help you position the pattern pieces on the glass so they will flow with the grain.

Using the Glass Grain to Advantage:

- The grain in a window should always follow the longest direction of the window. For example, if your panel is 36" tall and 12" wide, run the grain vertically. If you are making a transom 12" tall and 36" wide, run the grain horizontally. This design principle applies to the border pieces of a design as well.
- When you are making a floral or wildlife window, it's best to imitate nature as closely as possible. For example, on a flower the grain would run from the center of the flower out.

Copper Foil Method

Stained glass flat panels as well as three-dimensional objects like lampshades and boxes can be made using the copper foil method. After the glass is cut and fitted to the pattern, the glass pieces are wrapped with foil tape then joined together with solder. This method is a good method to learn if you are just starting out in glass crafting.

The copper foil projects in this section include flat panels, a frame, lampshades, boxes, and other tabletop accessories. Each project includes one or more photographs, a list of supplies you'll need, and step-by-step instructions for cutting, assembling, and finishing. Before you start any project in this section, review the techniques described and photographed in the basic instructions for the Copper Foil Method.

Basic Supplies for the Copper Foil Method

The following supplies are a check list of items you will need for creating projects using this crafting method. These supplies and tools have been pictured and explained in the chapter entitled "Supplies for Getting Started."

Pattern Making Supplies:

- Pattern fixative or rubber cement
- Pencil and eraser
- Felt-tip pen or china marker
- Pattern paper
- 18" metal ruler with cork back
- Transfer and tracing paper
- Colored pencils
- Pattern shears

Glass Cutting Tools:

- Glass cutter
- Lubricating oil
- Carborundum stone or emery cloth
  Optional: Grinder
- Breaking pliers
- Running pliers
- Grozing pliers
  Optional: Combination pliers

Assembly Supplies:

- Work board
- Squaring bars
- Push pins
- Triangle with 45 and 90 degree angles
- Desk brush and dust pan for cleanup
- Masking tape
- Cloth for wiping edges

Soldering Supplies:

- Solder
- Soldering iron with 1/4" tip
- Rheostat
- Soldering iron stand
- Tip cleaner
- Flux and flux brush

Safety gear:

- Safety glasses
- Face mask

Additional Supplies

In addition to the basic supplies listed previously, you will need some items that are specific to this type of crafting method.

Foil Tape

Foil tape is wrapped around each piece of glass before soldering. One side of the tape is smooth; the other side is sticky. The sticky side goes towards the edge of your glass. Available in copper or silver, foil tape is sold in various widths. The width needed for each project is specified in the individual project instructions.

Burnisher

A **foilmate** is a specialized tool with a roller on one end and a slot on the other. It is used to burnish the foil tape against the glass and create a tight bond.

You can also burnish foil tape with a wooden chopstick, a craft stick, an orange peeler, or a lathekin.

Craft Knife

Use a **craft knife** fitted with a #11 blade to cut foil tape.

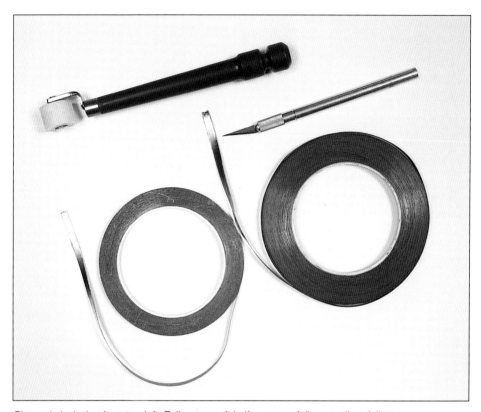

Pictured clockwise from top left: Foilmate, craft knife, copper foil tape, silver foil tape.

Crafting with Copper Foil

In this section, you'll see how to cut out a pattern, cut glass, use a grinder, put on copper foil, solder, and frame the finished project for display.

Step 1 • Prepare Your Pattern

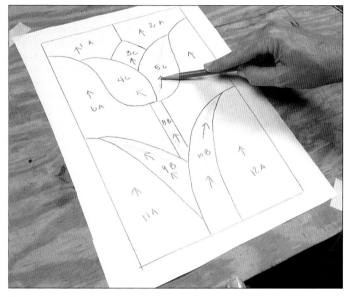

1. Position tracing paper over the pattern and trace the design lines with a pencil. Use arrows to mark the desired direction of the grain of the glass on the pattern. You will want the grain of the glass running in the same direction, no matter the color, so you need to add grain arrows.

Once the pattern pieces are cut out, it is often hard to determine the top from bottom or where they are within a design. It's a good habit to number the pattern pieces so they can be matched with the assembly pattern after cutting. I also add a letter after each number to indicate pattern pieces of a similar color. For example "A" might be the background color; "B" could be the flower color.

2. Transfer the design using transfer paper to white pattern paper or photocopy the traced design. You want to have two copies of the pattern—one to cut apart to make templates for cutting the glass and another to use as a guide when assembling the piece.

3. Color-code the pattern with colored pencils that correspond with glass colors you've chosen. This makes it easier to identify the pattern pieces after you've cut them apart to make the templates.

4. Cut the outside edges of pattern, using a ruler and a craft knife to get a clean, straight edge.

5. Use pattern shears to cut out the pattern pieces you will use as cutting templates. Put the single blade up toward you and start cutting with small strokes, not big ones. Hold your paper in your other hand and cut right along the line. Continue cutting until you have cut out every piece of your pattern. It doesn't matter the order you cut it out in; do whatever seems easiest for you.

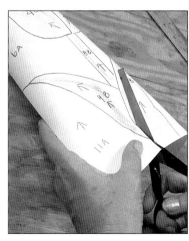

Step 2 • Cutting Glass Pieces

Caution! Always wear safety glasses to protect your eyes when cutting glass.

1. Determine how much glass you will need to cut your first piece by positioning the pattern piece on the glass. Divide the larger piece into a smaller, more manageable piece that will be enough to cut all of the pieces of that color. Score that piece of glass from the larger piece, using your glass cutter.

To break the glass, pick it up and put your fingers under the glass and your thumbs on top. Rock your hands up and away from you. The glass will break along the scored line.

2. Apply pattern fixative or rubber cement to the backs of the pattern pieces. Position the pattern pieces on the right (smooth) side of glass, aligning the arrows you marked on the pattern pieces with the grain of the glass. Allow 1/4"-1/2" all around each piece to make breaking out the pieces easier. *Option:* If you have a light box, you can place the pattern on the light box and position the glass over the pattern. The pattern lines will be visible through the glass. Use a china marker or felt-tip marker (one that's not permanent on glass) to transfer the pattern lines to the glass.

3. To begin cutting the first pattern piece, start the cut at the edge of the piece of glass and move the cutter to the edge of the pattern template.

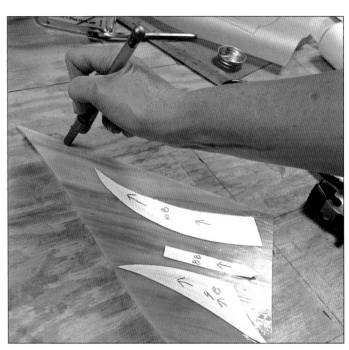

4. Continue the cut along the edge of the pattern template. This photo shows how to hold the cutting tool properly. Note the placement of the fingers and thumb and the angle of the cutting tool in relation to the glass.

5. Finish the cut by continuing past the edge of the pattern template and off the edge of the glass.

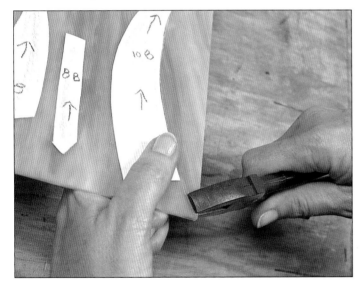

6. Break the glass with breaking pliers, holding the glass surface in one hand and holding the pliers in your other hand. Position the edge of the pliers on the scored line. Breaking pliers work well on curved cuts. Use the same technique to score and break the other two sides of the piece—scoring, then breaking; scoring, then breaking. Always score the inside curves first, then the outside curves. Score straight lines last.

7. Use running pliers on straight cuts, like this stem piece. Score the glass from one edge to the other along the pattern template's edge. Align the mark on the running pliers with the scored line to break the glass.

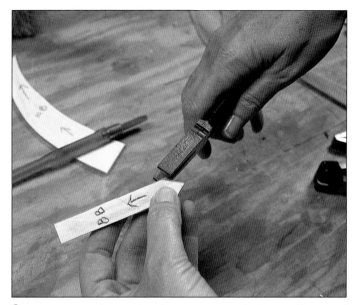

8. Use grozing pliers to break away any small chips or flanges of glass that protrude on the edges of cut pieces. You will save a lot of time if you use your grozing pliers to remove most of the unwanted glass before you go to the grinder. **TIP:** To ensure a clean work surface, periodically sweep off your work surface with a brush to remove small chips and slivers of glass that accumulate as you work.

9. To cut deep curves, make successive scores and breaks to gradually move into the final cut. The dotted lines show how this background piece could be scored and separated.

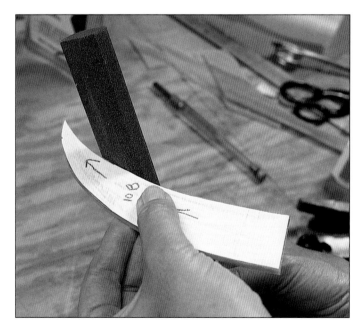

10. Smooth the edges of each cut piece with a carborundum stone or a piece of emery cloth.

11. Or use an electric grinder to smooth the edges. Keep the pattern pieces attached to the glass as you work on the edges.

Step 3 • Assembling the Project

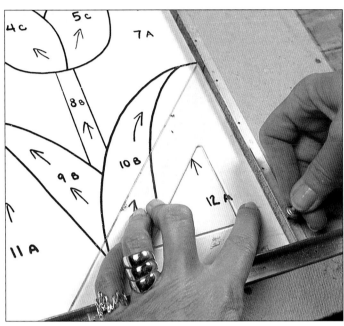

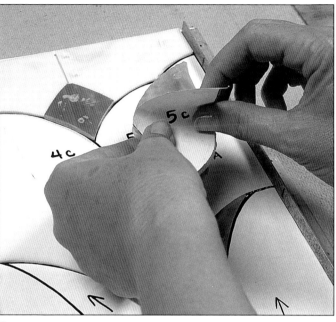

1. Set up your work space by first placing the intact pattern on the surface. Your glass pieces will be assembled on top of this pattern. Place the squaring bars around three sides of the intact copy of your pattern. Use a triangle to be sure the bars are perfectly square. Leave one end open for moving the pieces in and out.

2. Working one piece at a time, remove the pattern template from the cut glass piece and position the piece over the appropriate part of the pattern.

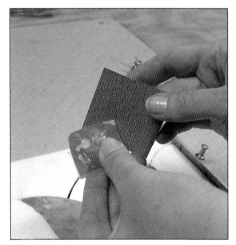

3. Continue positioning until all pieces are in place.

4. If the pieces are too tight or don't fit well, use a piece of emery cloth or an electric grinder to work on the edges and reduce the size of the piece.

5. When all pieces are fit and placed, add the last squaring bar and secure in place. Leave the pieces within the squaring bars during the foiling process, picking up only one piece at a time to apply the foil tape. Otherwise, the pieces might not fit together.

Step 4 • Foiling the Glass Pieces

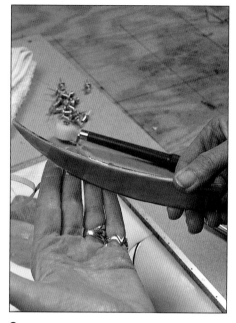

1. Wipe the edges of all the glass pieces with a cloth to remove any oil residue from the glass cutter and all the powder from the grinder or carborundum stone.

2. Pull the backing paper from the end of the roll of foil tape and position the edge of the glass piece on the foil, centering the edge of the glass piece on the tape.

3. Keep applying foil tape around the piece to cover ALL the edges of the piece. Keep the piece centered on the foil so the foil overlaps the piece equally on both sides. (This is the easiest part of doing stained glass. If you're making a big project like a lampshade, you may have to apply foil to as many as a thousand pieces—it's time consuming, but not difficult.)

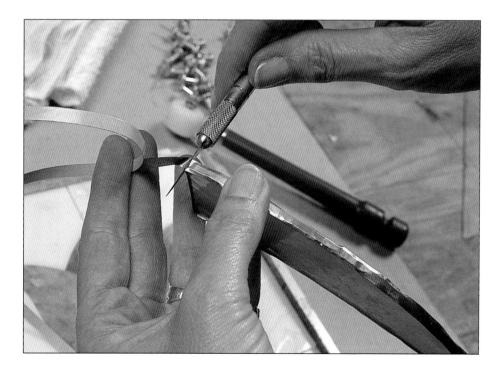

4. When all the edges of a piece have been covered and you get to the place where you started, overlap the foil tape slightly—about 1/4"—and cut the end of the foil tape with a craft knife.

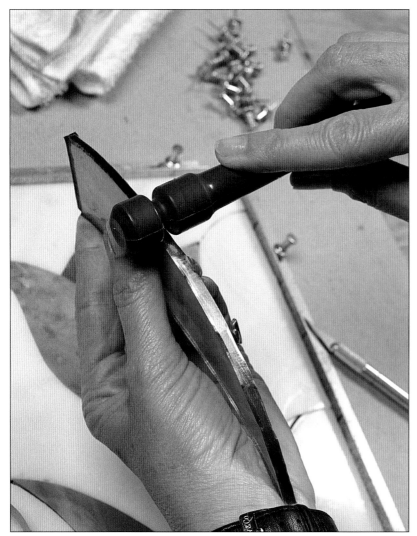

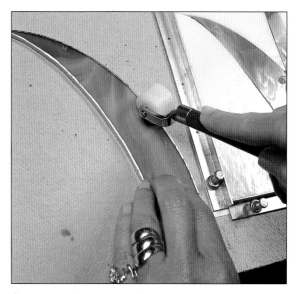

6. Burnish the tape to the sides of the glass piece to secure the foil, using the roller end of the burnisher. Be sure to burnish both sides of the glass piece. If you have done a good job, you won't be able to see where you overlapped the beginning and end of the foil and you won't be able to feel a ridge between the glass and the foil. It should be perfectly smooth on the edges.

5. Burnish the tape on the edge of glass for a smooth, secure bond. Run the grooved end of the foilmate around the edge of the glass to press the tape securely against the edge. **Don't** run your fingers along the edge of the glass—that's a good way to get a foil cut.

7. Continue the foiling process until foil tape has been applied to all pieces. Work one piece at a time, replacing each piece within the squaring bars after you apply the foil tape.

Step 5 • Soldering Glass Pieces

Caution: Always solder in an area with adequate ventilation. Soldering fumes are not healthy to breathe.

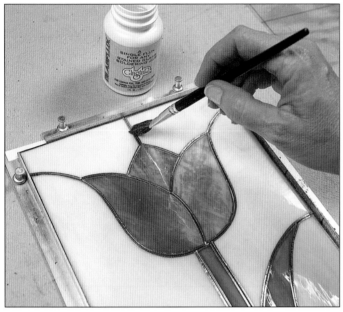

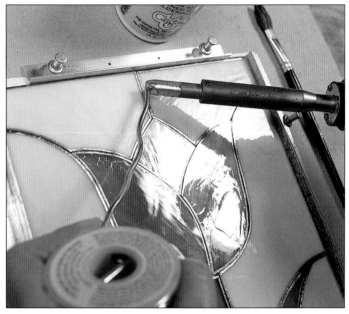

1. Heat soldering iron. Brush flux on the first area you plan to solder. You do not have to be precise. Make sure you cover the foil. It is okay if you get some flux on the glass.

2. Position the tip of the soldering iron over the foiled area, holding the iron in one hand and the roll of solder in the other hand. Hold the solder wire against the iron to melt the solder as you move the iron along.

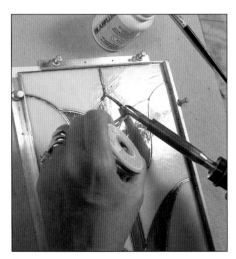

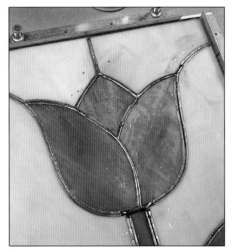

5. When you've completed one side of the piece, turn it over and solder the other side. **TIP:** If you notice drip-through on the other side when you turn over the piece, take a wet cloth and lay it underneath the piece as you work. That will cool the solder more quickly and stop drip-throughs from seeping to the other side.

3. Draw the tip of the soldering iron along the flux-brushed foil, melting solder as you go. The solder will stay on the metal area and resist the glass.

4. Continue to solder, working one area at a time—first applying flux, then soldering. For a smooth bead of solder at joints where pieces intersect, run the solder a short way in each direction from the joint.

Step 6 • Framing the Piece

Panels will need to be stabilized on the edges with a came frame. Even if you are going to frame your piece with a wooden or metal frame, I like to add came around a piece to strengthen it.

See "Lead Came Method" beginning on page 80 for information about using came.

1. When you've finished soldering and have removed the squaring bars, measure each side of the piece to determine how much U-shaped came you need to frame the panel, working clockwise. Add the measurements together for each side to get a measurement for the total length of came needed. For example, if you have an 8" x 10" panel, you will need a piece of came 36" long (8" + 8" + 10" + 10").

2. Mark each measurement **in order—working clockwise** on a length of U-shaped came with a felt-tip marker. The marks indicate where the came will be notched so the piece of came will fold around the edges of the panel, forming mitered corners. For example, for an 8" x 10" vertical piece—mark 8", then 10", then 8", then 10".

3. Notch the came at the places you have marked, using a came notcher.

4. Place the U-shaped came around the panel, bending the came at the notches and positioning the notches at the corners. Use push pins to hold the came in place around the panel.

5. Brush flux on the joint where the two ends of the came come together at one corner and solder. Remember to brush flux on the joint before soldering. When you have soldered one side, turn the panel over and solder the joint on the other side.

6. Optional: You can create little eyes of wire for hanging you panel. Use roundnose pliers to form circles of aluminum wire. Solder a wire circle at each side of the panel on the back. Attach monofilament line through the loops to hang the panel.

Notching the came for mitering.

Placing notched came around edge of panel.

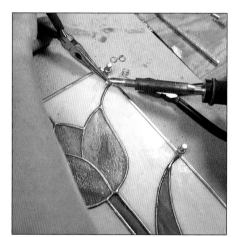

Soldering end joint.

Mallard Duck Panel

My Uncle Denny has always been an outdoorsman. He is particularly fond of ducks, so when some friends acquired an original Tiffany jewel press and gave me two cattail jewels, I had to design this panel for Denny. It has always been one of my favorite projects and has appeared in several of my television shows and videos.

If you do not want to use a wooden frame, substitute zinc came for the lead. Hang with eye hooks.

MALLARD
BY. VICKI PAYNE

Size: 20" x 16"

Supplies

Glass:
Background, 3 sq. ft.
Various shades of gray and white, 1 sq.
   ft. *each*
Green iridized ripple, 1/2 sq. ft.
Smooth green, 1/2 sq. ft.
Yellow, 1/2 sq. ft.
2 cattail jewels *or* brown glass

Metals:
Copper foil tape, 3/16"
1 six-foot strip of 3/8" H lead came

Tools & Other Supplies:
Oak frame
Screw-in hooks
Basic Tools & Supplies for Copper Foil
   Method

Step-by-Step

Prepare, Cut & Assemble:
1. Enlarge pattern to desired size and make an extra copy. Number and color-code each piece.
2. Using pattern shears, cut out one copy of the pattern.
3. Adhere cut pattern piece to glass. Cut out each piece.
4. On your work board, tape or pin the second copy of the pattern. Lay out and fit glass pieces to the pattern. Use your glass grinder to make adjustments. Clean all glass edges.

Apply Foil & Solder:
1. Wrap each piece of glass with 3/16" foil.
2. Solder all the pieces together, building up a nice smooth bead along the solder seams.
3. Turn over the project and solder the back side the same as the front. Keep the solder joints low around the outside edges of the panel so the lead came frame will fit easily on the glass.

Finish:
1. Slip the came on the four sides of the panel and hold in place with horseshoe nails. Make sure the lead frame is squared.
2. Secure the lead to the panel by soldering at each foil/lead intersection.
3. Turn over the panel and solder the intersections on the back.
4. Clean up with soap and water.
5. *Option:* Apply patina (see page 97).
6. Frame with wood. ❀

Enlarge to 235% for actual size

Rosebud Panel

A single rosebud is a perfect subject for stained glass. The ripple glass selected for the rosebud provides an appropriate texture for a rose yet to be unfurled. I used confetti/streamer glass for the background area around the rose to give the illusion of garden foliage.

The copper patina used on the foil seams and the copper came framing provided a warm contrast to the white background glass.

Size: 11" x 19"

Supplies

Glass:
White glass, 2 sq. ft. (for background)
Confetti/streamer glass, 1 sq. ft
Green/red opalescent glass, 1 sq. ft.
Red ripple glass, 1/2 sq. ft.
Green glass, 1/2 sq. ft. (for leaves)
Brown glass, 1/2 sq. ft. (for stem)

Metals:
Copper foil tape, 3/16"
1 6-ft. strip of 1/2" copper U came
2 copper eye hooks, 1/2"

Tools & Other Supplies:
Copper patina (see page 97)
Basic Tools & Supplies for the Copper
    Foil Method
Came saw *or* hacksaw

Step by Step

Prepare, Cut & Assemble:
1. Enlarge pattern to desired size and make an extra copy.
2. Using pattern shears, cut out one copy of the pattern.
3. Cut out glass pieces.
4. On your work board, tape or pin the second copy of the pattern. Lay out and fit glass pieces to the pattern. Use your glass grinder to make any adjustments.
5. Using a came saw or hacksaw, cut copper came to size.

Apply Foil & Solder:
1. Wrap pieces with 3/16" foil.
2. Solder all the pieces together and build up a nice smooth bead along the solder seams. Keep the solder joints low around the outside edges of the panel so the came will fit easily on the glass.
3. Turn the project over and solder the back.

Finish:
1. Insert the eye hooks in the outside channel of the side pieces of copper framing. Solder firmly in place.
2. Slip the came on the four sides of the panel and hold in place with horseshoe nails. Make sure the copper frame is squared.
3. Secure the came to the panel by soldering at each foil/came intersection.
4. Turn over the panel and solder the intersections on the back side.
5. Clean up with soap and water.
6. Apply copper patina according to patina manufacturer's instructions. ❀

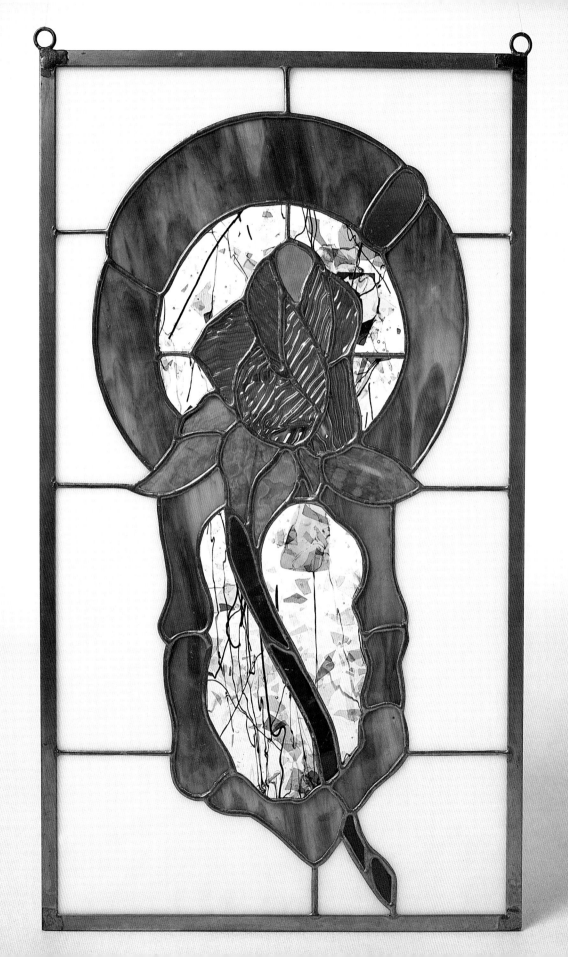

*Enlarge to 215%
for actual size*

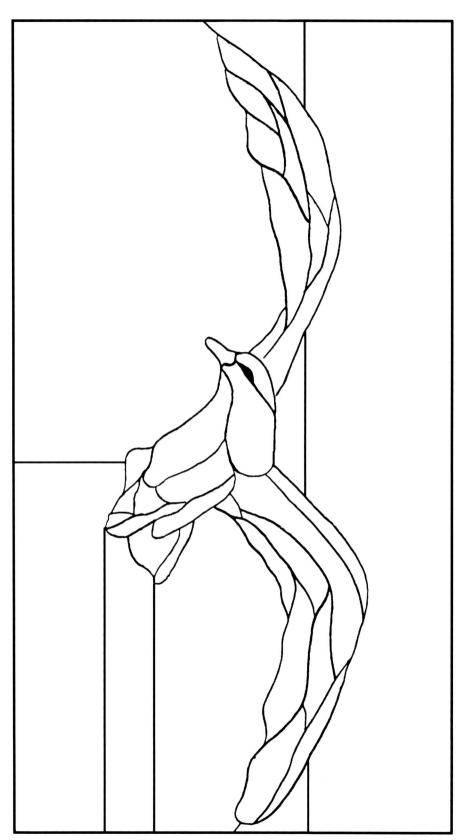

*Instructions begin
on page 40*

*Enlarge to 270%
for actual size*

Seagull Panel

Working from a photograph I took during a family trip to the beach, I created this light and airy stained glass panel. When you make it, recall your memories of the beach.

Size: 23" x 12-1/2"
Pattern on page 39

Supplies

Glass:
Blue water glass, 3 sq. ft. (for the background)
Assortment of light gray, black, and white glasses, 1/2 sq. ft. of each

Metals:
Copper foil tape, 3/16"
1 6-ft. strip of 1/2" U zinc came
2 eye hooks, 1/2"

Tools & Other Supplies:
Basic Tools & Supplies for Copper Foil Method
Came saw *or* hacksaw

Step-by-Step

Prepare, Cut & Assemble:
1. Enlarge pattern and make an extra copy.
2. Using pattern shears, cut out one copy of the pattern.
3. Adhere pattern pieces to the glass and cut out each piece.
4. On your work board, tape or pin the other copy of the pattern. Lay out and fit glass pieces to the pattern. Use your glass grinder to make any adjustments.
5. Using a came saw or hacksaw, cut zinc came to size.

Apply Foil & Solder:
1. Apply 3/16" foil to all pieces.
2. Solder the pieces together, building up a nice smooth bead along the solder seams. Keep the solder joints low around the outside edges of the panel so the zinc came will fit easily on the glass.
3. Turn over the project and solder the back side.

Finish:

1. Insert the eye hooks in the outside channels of the side pieces of the zinc came frame. Solder firmly in place.
2. Slip the zinc came on the four sides of the panel and hold in place with horseshoe nails. Make sure the zinc frame is squared.
3. Secure the zinc to the panel by soldering at each place the foil seam intersects the zinc came frame.
4. Turn over the panel and solder at the intersections on the other side.
5. Clean up with soap and water. ✿

Sailboat Wind Chime

Size: 8" x 10-3/4"

Supplies

Glass:
White opalescent glass, 1 sq. ft.
Yellow opalescent glass, 1/2 sq. ft.
Orange opalescent glass, 6" square
Blue opalescent glass, 6" square

Metals:
Copper foil tape, 7/32"
12 gauge copper wire

Tools & Other Supplies:
Black patina
Clear nylon filament fishing line
Basic Tools & Supplies for Copper Foil
    Method
Needlenose pliers

Step-by-Step

Prepare, Cut & Assemble:
1. Enlarge pattern and make an extra copy.
2. Using pattern shears, cut out one copy of the pattern.
3. Cut out the sailboat pieces. Cut out five fish, using the colors shown in the project photo.
4. On your work board, tape or pin down the second copy of the pattern. Lay out and fit glass pieces to the pattern. Use your glass grinder to make any adjustments.

Apply Foil & Solder:
1. Apply 3/16" foil to all the pieces.
2. Secure foiled pieces in place with push pins.

3. Form flag holder and fish holder with copper wire, using the pattern provided. Secure in place.
4. Solder the pieces together, building up a nice smooth bead along the solder seams.
5. Turn over the pieces and solder the back side.

Finish:
1. Clean up with soap and water.
2. Apply patina according to manufacturer's instructions.
3. Assemble the wind chime by securing the fish to the fish holder with clear fishing line. Add another piece of fishing line to the flag wire for hanging. ✲

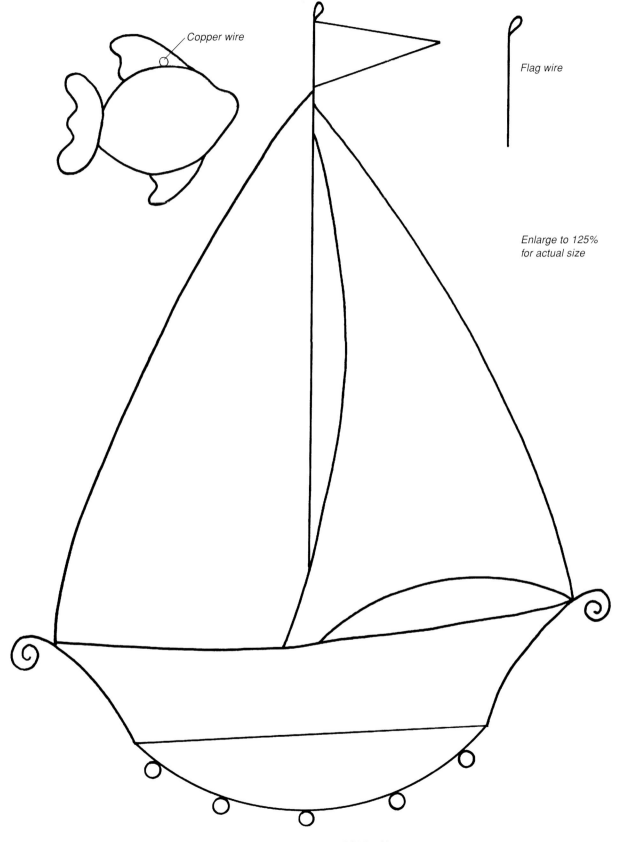

Copper wire

Flag wire

Enlarge to 125%
for actual size

Snowflakes

Even if you don't love snow, you can't help but love these sparkling snowflakes by designer Deverie Wood. These beautiful projects will brighten any winter or summer day. You can use standard-size pre-cut bevels or work with textured art glass.

Size: Larger snowflake - 15" x 15"
Smaller snowflake - 6" x 6"

Supplies

Glass:
For larger snowflake:
Gold dichroic glass, 1 sq. ft.
Clear iridized ripple glass, 1/2 sq. ft.
30 medium-size clear iridized glass nuggets

For smaller snowflake:
6 diamond-shape clear glass bevels
6 curved-diamond clear glass bevels
6 medium-size clear glass nuggets
12 small blue glass nuggets

Metals:
Black-backed copper foil tape, 3/16"

Tools & Other Supplies:
Black patina
Basic Tools & Supplies for Copper Foil Method

Step-by-Step

The procedure for making both snowflakes is the same, but for the smaller snowflake, no cutting is required—you simply apply the foil to the beveled pieces and the nuggets and solder.

1. Enlarge pattern and make an extra copy.
2. Cut out one copy of the pattern.
3. Adhere pattern pieces to the glass and cut out each piece.
4. On your work board, tape or pin down the other copy of the pattern. Lay out and fit the glass pieces to the pattern. Use your glass grinder to make any adjustments.

Apply Foil & Solder:

1. Apply 3/16" foil to all the glass pieces. *Tip:* If you have trouble getting the foil to stick to the nuggets, pass the side edge of the nugget against your grinder bit. This will give the nugget a better edge for the foil.
2. Solder all the pieces together, building up a nice smooth bead over all inside and outside copper seams and edges.
3. Puddle solder the nuggets to the glass pieces.
4. Turn over the project and solder the back side the same as the front.

Finish:

1. Clean up with soap and water.
2. Apply patina according to manufacturer's instructions. ❊

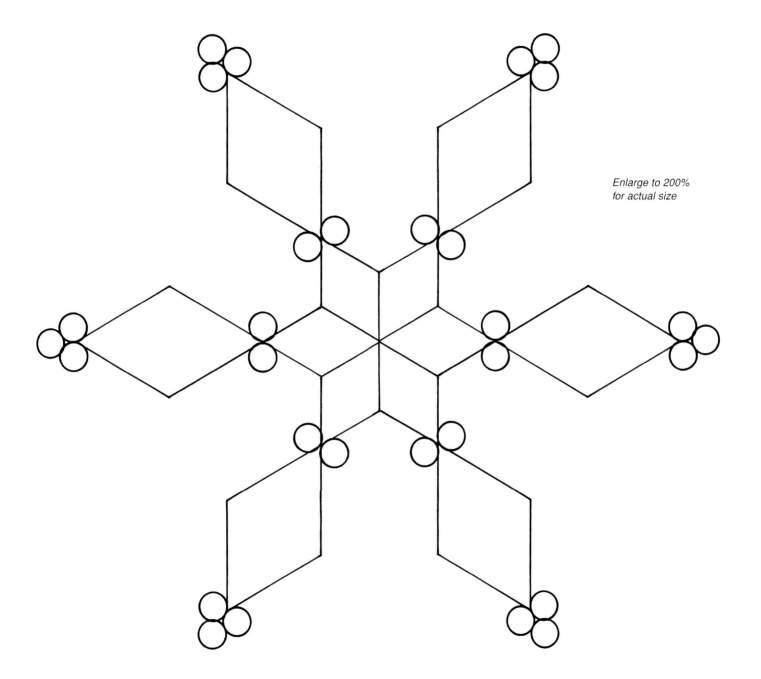

*Enlarge to 200%
for actual size*

Sweet Peas Panel

Veggies are fun subjects for glass projects. This little panel would brighten up anyone's kitchen window. Its fresh colors and clean lines are accented by three-dimensional glass nuggets used for the peas. The puddle soldering around these little jewels is easy to do.

Size: 10" x 12"

Supplies

Glass:
Amber opalescent glass, 1 sq. ft. (for background)

Green opalescent glass, 3 shades, 1/2 sq. ft.

12 medium green glass nuggets

Metals:
Copper foil tape, 3/16"

Copper foil tape, 7/32"

1 6-ft. strip of 1/8" U brass came

Tools & Other Supplies:
Basic Supplies for Copper Foil Method

Came notcher *or* tin snips

Optional: Black patina

Step-by-Step

Prepare, Cut & Assemble:
1. Enlarge pattern and make an extra copy.
2. Using pattern shears, cut out one copy of the pattern.
3. Adhere pattern pieces of the glass. Cut out each glass piece.
4. On your work board, tape or pin the other copy of the pattern. Lay out and fit glass pieces to the pattern. Use your glass grinder to make any adjustments.
5. Use your came notcher or tin snips to cut the U brass came to size.

Apply Foil & Solder:
1. Apply 3/16" foil to the edges of all the cut glass pieces.
2. Apply 7/32" foil to the edges of the nuggets. *TIP:* Grinding the edges of the nuggets will make it easier to adhere the foil tape.
3. Solder all the pieces together, building up a nice smooth bead along the solder seams. Keep the solder joints low around the outside edges of the panel so the came will fit easily on the glass.
4. Puddle solder around each nugget by feeding enough molten solder into the open spaces around the nugget and glass. If you have problems with molten solder running through to the back, place a damp cloth under the panel.
5. Turn over the project. Because the nuggets are thicker than the cut glass pieces, you will need to level the panel by placing a folded rag under the edges. Solder the back side.

Finish:
1. Slip the came on the four sides of the panel and hold in place with horseshoe nails. Make sure the frame is squared.
2. Secure the brass came to the panel by soldering at each foil/came intersection.
3. Turn over the panel and solder the intersections on the back.
4. Clean up with soap and water.
5. *Option:* Apply patina according to manufacturer's instructions. ❀

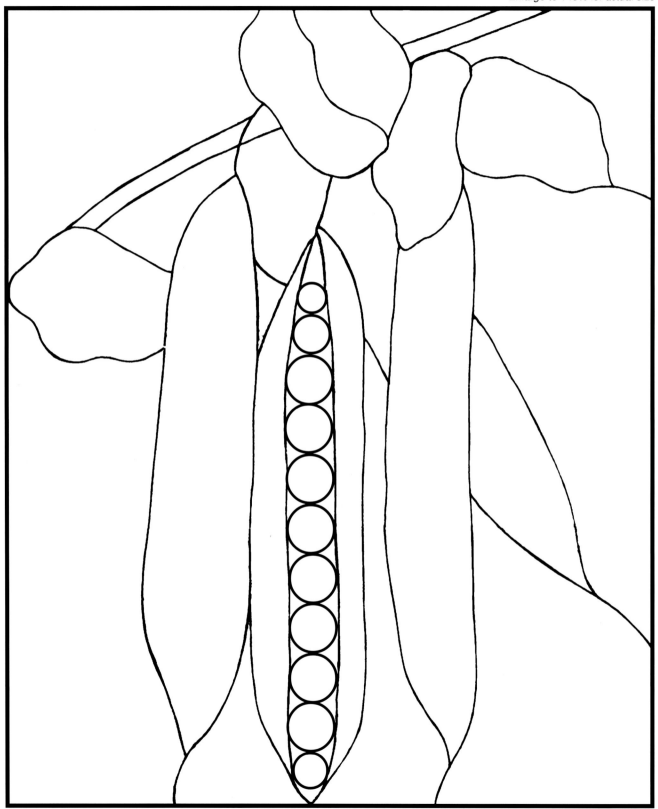

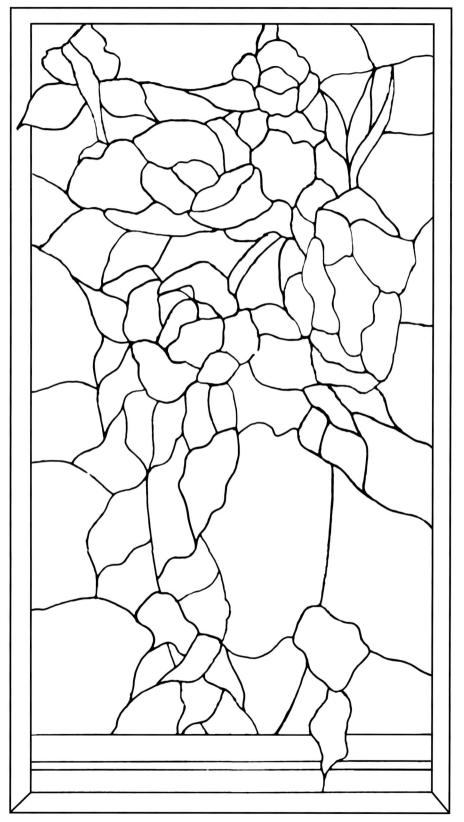

Enlarge to 317% for actual size

Instructions begin on page 50.

Vase of Roses Panel

Roses are one of my favorite flowers—I love cutting fresh ones from my garden and arranging them in beautiful glass vases. I designed this project around that activity. I used a beautiful piece of purple drapery glass for the vase and mixed a combination of various shades of red and white glasses to create the flowers. The background has just the hint of yellow like a sunny day in the garden.

Size: 15" x 27"
Pattern on page 49

Supplies

Glass:
Pale yellow and white glass, 3 sq. ft. (for background)
Purple drapery glass, 1 sq. foot
White glass, 1 sq. ft.
Red glass, various shades, 1 sq. ft.
Green glass, various shades, 1 sq. ft.

Metals:
Copper foil tape, 3/16"
Copper foil tape, 7/32" or wider, depending on thickness of the drapery glass
1 6-ft. strip of 3/4" brass U came
2 eye hooks, 1/2"

Tools & Other Supplies:
Basic Tools & Supplies for Copper Foil Method
Came saw *or* hacksaw
Optional: Black patina

Step-by-Step

Prepare, Cut & Assemble:
1. Enlarge the pattern and make an extra copy.
2. Using pattern shears, cut out one copy of the pattern.
3. Adhere the pattern pieces to the glass. Cut out the glass pieces.
4. On your work board, tape or pin the other copy of the pattern. Lay out and fit glass pieces to the pattern. Use your glass grinder to make any adjustments.
5. Using a came saw or hacksaw, cut brass came to size.

Apply Foil & Solder:
1. Apply 3/16" foil tape to the edges of all the pieces except the drapery glass. Use 7/32" (or wider) foil on the drapery glass.
2. Solder all the pieces together, building up a nice smooth bead along the solder seams. Keep the solder joints low around the outside edges so the brass came will fit easily on the glass.
3. Turn over the panel and solder the back.

Finish:
1. Insert the eye hooks in the outside channel of the two side pieces of the brass came frame. Solder firmly in place.
2. Slip the brass came on the four sides of the panel and hold in place with horseshoe nails.
3. Secure the brass came to the panel by soldering at each foil/came intersection.
4. Turn over the panel and solder the foil/came intersections on the back.
5. Clean up with soap and water.
6. *Option:* Apply patina according to manufacturer's instructions. ❈

Yellow Rose Panel

Growing up in Texas, one of the first songs I learned to sing was "The Yellow Rose of Texas," and this yellow rose was one of the first panels I designed when I started working with art glass. It's still one of my favorites and is now part of our Certified Teacher's Program. (If you're not from Texas, be forewarned that this little panel is so much fun to make that you could end up talking with a "twang.")

Size: 12" x 9"
Pattern on page 54

Supplies

Glass:
Clear double glue chip, 1 sq. ft. (for the
   background)
Yellow opalescent, 1 sq. ft.
Light green opalescent, 3 sq. in.
Green opalescent, 1/2 sq. ft.

Metals:
Copper foil tape, 3/16"
1 6-ft. strip of 1/2" U zinc came
12 gauge copper wire

Tools & Other Supplies:
Optional: Black patina
Came saw *or* hacksaw
Basic Tools & Supplies for Copper Foil
   Method

Step by Step

Prepare, Cut & Assemble:

1. Enlarge pattern to desired size and make an extra copy. Number and color-code each piece. Using pattern shears, cut out one copy of the pattern.
2. Adhere cut pattern pieces to glass. Cut out glass pieces.
3. On your work board, tape or pin the second copy of the pattern. Lay out and fit glass pieces to the pattern. Use your glass grinder to make any adjustments.
4. Using a came saw or hacksaw, cut zinc to size.

Apply Foil & Solder:

1. Wrap each piece in 3/16" foil.
2. Solder all the pieces together, building up a nice smooth bead along the solder seams. Keep the solder joints low around the outside edges of the panel so the zinc came will fit easily on the glass.
3. Turn over the project and solder the back the same as the front.

Finish:

1. Slip the zinc came on the four sides of the panel and hold in place with horseshoe nails. Make sure the zinc frame is squared.
2. Secure the zinc to the panel by soldering at each foil/came intersection.
3. Turn over the panel over and solder the intersections on the back.
4. Using round nose pliers, make two loops of copper wire. On the back, solder loops to the top corners of the panel.
5. Clean up with soap and water.
6. *Option:* Apply patina according to manufacturer's instructions. ❂

Enlarge to 171% for actual size

Purple Iris Panel

This iris design is a wonderful use for beautiful opalescent glass.

Size: 8-3/8" x 11-1/4"

Supplies

Glass:
Amber opalescent, 1 sq. ft. (for the background)
Green opalescent, 1/2 sq. ft.
Purple opalescent, 1/2 sq. ft.
Yellow, 2 sq. in.

Metals:
Copper foil tape, 3/16"
1 6-ft. strip of 1/2" U zinc came
12 gauge copper wire

Tools & Other Supplies:
Black patina
Basic Tools & Supplies for Copper Foil Method
Pliers

Step-by-Step

Prepare, Cut & Assemble:

1. Enlarge pattern to desired size and make an extra copy. Number and color-code each piece. Using pattern shears, cut out one copy of the pattern.
2. Adhere cutout pattern pieces to the glass. Cut out glass pieces.
3. On your work board, tape or pin down the second copy of the pattern. Attach squaring strips to keep the panel squared up as you work.
4. Lay out and fit glass pieces to the pattern. Use your glass grinder to make any adjustments.

5. Using a came saw or hack-saw, cut zinc came to size.

Apply Foil & Solder:

1. Wrap glass pieces with 3/16" foil.
2. Solder all the pieces together, building up a nice smooth bead along the solder seams. Keep the solder joints low around the outside edges of the panel so the zinc came will fit easily on the glass.
3. Turn over the project and solder the back side the same way.

Finish:

1. Slip the zinc came on the four sides of the panel and hold in place with horseshoe nails. Make sure the zinc frame is squared.
2. Secure the came to the panel by soldering at each foil/came intersection.
3. Turn over the panel and solder the intersections on the back.
4. Using round nose pliers, make two loops of copper wire. On the back, solder the loops to the top corners of the panel.
5. Clean up with soap and water.
6. *Option:* Apply patina according to manufacturer's instructions. ✿

Enlarge to 150% for actual size

Lampshade with Bead Trim

Stained glass, one of the oldest forms of craftsmanship, can easily be adapted to today's latest trends. Beads and wire update this simple little panel lamp to fit in any décor. This is a great first time panel lamp project. Select the color that coordinates with your taste and have fun accenting it with your favorite beads and colored wire.

I like to make my patterns for cutting lamp pieces out of Mylar®, a frosted plastic film that doesn't shrink during grinding and repeated use so I only need one copy of each pattern piece.

Size: 7" x 6-3/4"

Supplies

Glass:
Pink opalescent glass, 7" x 20"
Green opalescent glass, 2-1/2" x 10"
4 colorful glass beads

Metals:
Copper foil tape, 7/32"
Copper wire
3-1/4" octagonal brass vase cap

Other Tools & Supplies:
Lamp base of your choice
Basic Tools & Supplies for Copper Foil
    Method
Vase cap
Optional: Mylar® sheets, black patina,
    double-sided tape

Step-by-Step

Prepare, Cut & Apply Foil:
1. Make 8 paper copies (or one Mylar® copy) of the pattern. Cut out pattern piece(s), using pattern shears.
2. Adhere pattern(s) to the glass. If using a Mylar® pattern, it can be adhered to glass with double-sided tape. Cut out each piece.
3. Grind edges of each piece as needed to fit the pattern. Clean all glass edges.

4. Wrap each piece of glass in 7/32" copper foil.

Assemble:
1. Lay out the pink glass panels on your work surface, right side down. (**Note:** The green "leaves" will be added later.) Check closely to make sure you haven't flipped a panel the wrong way. Keep the top and the bottom edges of each panel even with those of the next panel. (Photo 1)
2. Criss-cross masking tape over the back of each panel, making sure your tape adheres firmly to the panels. The

more tape you use, the easier the shade will be to assemble. (Photo 2) Cut four or five additional pieces of masking tape and have them ready for the next step.
3. Flip the assembly so that the righ sides of the panels are face up. Holding the top edges of the two outside panels, lift the top of the shade up and off the table and into its upright position. Secure the two end panels with tape where they meet. Adjust the shape, and secure with more tape. (Photo 3)

Instructions continue on page 58.

How to Assemble a Panel Shade

1. Lay out pieces, right sides down, on your work surface.

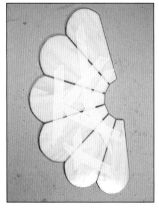

2. Tape pieces together on the back, criss-crossing the tape strips as shown.

3. Hold upright and adjust the shape, and secure with tape before soldering.

Solder the Shade:

1. Apply the flux to the copper foil along the top of the shade and tack solder each panel to the adjacent panel.
2. Gently rotate the shade and stand it on its neck. **NEVER lay the shade on its side**—doing that will flatten the shade and pull the foil from the glass.
3. With the shade in this position, check the bottoms of the panels and adjust the shape as needed. Turn the shade to its original position. Fill each seam, from top to bottom, with solder. Don't be concerned with looks for now - you just want to make sure the shade is sturdy and will hold its shape during the beading stage.
4. Using a cardboard box or sandbags, position the shade so it is level. (Fig. 1) Make sure the shade is secure and there is no pressure moving it out of shape.
5. Apply flux to one seam and solder a smooth, level bead of solder. Allow this seam to cool. Rotate the shade to expose the next seam.
   - If the hot solder drips through the seam, turn down the temperature of your iron.
   - If your seam is pasty and lumpy looking, turn up the temperature.
   - If you still have difficulty, move to another seam and allow the problem area to cool down.

6. When you have soldered all the outside seams, lay the shade on its side and solder the inside seams.

Attach Beads & Leaves:

1. Cut four pieces of copper wire, each 4" long. Thread one glass bead on each piece of wire, leaving 1" of wire above the bead. Form the lower wire into a spiral or other shape.
2. Lay two glass "leaf" pieces, right side down, on a 4" piece of masking tape, with the 1" of copper wire above the bead positioned between the two pieces of glass. Tack solder the two glass pieces and wire together. Repeat for remaining leaf pairs and beads.
3. Secure the two leaf-and-bead clusters to the lamp with masking tape, using the photo as a guide for placement. Solder in place.

Reinforce the Shade:

All shades should be reinforced with copper wire for additional support and durability.

1. Measure the top and bottom circumferences of the shade. Add the two measurements and cut copper wire to those lengths.

2. Stretch the wire before you use it—stretching gives the wire additional strength and removes any twists or kinks.
3. Tack solder the wire around the top and bottom of shade. (Fig. 2)
4. Apply additional solder to cover the wire, making the edges as smooth as possible.

Attach Vase Cap:

1. Position the vase cap on top of the shade. Make sure it is level. Secure with masking tape.
2. Turn over the shade and, working from the inside, solder the cap to the neck support wire and vertical foil seams. Solder it securely; this area will receive the most stress over the years.

Finish:

1. Wash your lampshade with warm soapy water. (You can place the shade directly in a utility-type sink for cleaning.) Drain and dry the shade.
2. *Option:* Apply black patina according to the manufacturer's instructions.
3. Polish or buff the shade with glass wax or polish. ✹

Fig. 1 - Supporting the shade for soldering with a cardboard box.

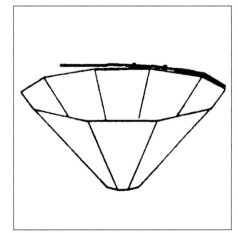

Fig. 2 - Reinforcing the bottom of the shade with wire.

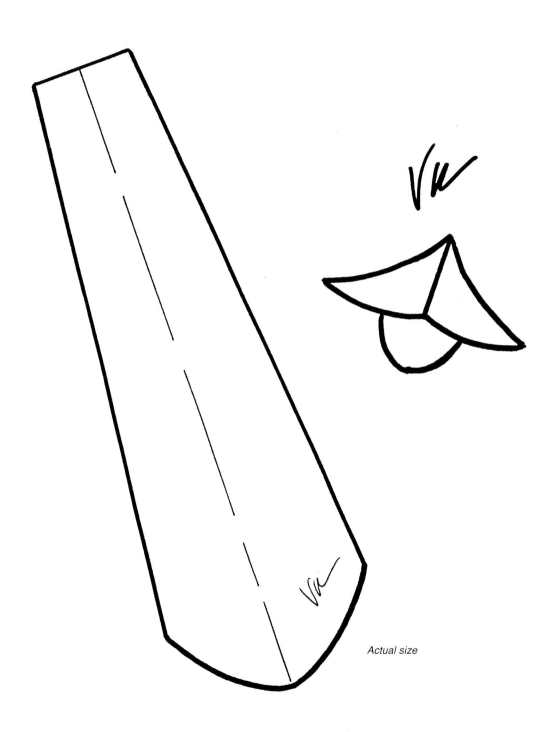

Actual size

Victorian Lampshade with Fringe

Size: 11-5/8" diameter

Supplies

Glass:
Pink opalescent glass, 10" x 24"

Metals:
Copper foil tape, 3/16"
Copper wire
3-1/2" brass vase cap

Tools & Other Supplies:
Lamp base of your choice
1 yd. bead fringe
Black patina
Basic Tools & Supplies for Copper Foil
    Method
Jewelry glue
Vase cap
Optional: Mylar® sheet (for pattern),
    double-sided tape

Step-by-Step

Prepare, Cut & Apply Foil:
1. Enlarge pattern and make an extra copy.
2. Using pattern shears, cut out one copy of the pattern. *Option:* Make a Mylar® copy of each piece.
3. Cut out 12 pieces of glass from each of the three pattern pieces, 36 pieces in all.
4. Grind edges of each piece as needed to fit the pattern. Clean all glass edges.
5. Wrap each piece of glass in 3/16" copper foil.

Assemble & Solder:
Assemble and solder the top two rows of shade first. When complete add the bottom row.

Reinforce the Shade:
All shades should be reinforced with copper wire for additional support and durability.
1. Measure the top and bottom circumferences of the shade. Add the two measurements and cut copper wire to those lengths.
2. Stretch the wire before you use it—stretching gives the wire additional strength and removes any twists or kinks.
3. Tack solder the wire around the top and bottom of shade.
4. Apply additional solder to cover the wire, making the edges as smooth as possible.

Attach Vase Cap:
1. Position the vase cap on top of the shade. Make sure it is level. Secure with masking tape.
2. Turn over the shade and, working from the inside, solder the cap to the neck support wire and vertical foil seams. Solder it securely; this area will receive the most stress over the years.

Finish:
1. Wash your lampshade with warm soapy water. (You can place the shade directly in a utility-type sink for cleaning.) Drain and dry the shade.
2. *Option:* Apply black patina according to the manufacturer's instructions.
3. Polish or buff the shade with glass wax or polish.
4. Attach the beaded trim along the lower rim with jewelry glue. ✺

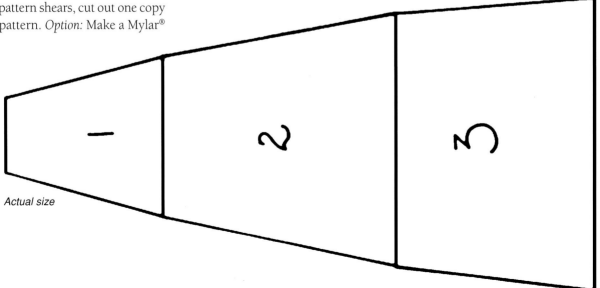

Actual size

Round Hummingbird Panel

This round panel has a shimmery water glass background.
Ladder chain is used to make an unusual, interesting frame.

Size: 9-1/4" diameter

Supplies

Glass:
Light blue water glass, 1 sq. ft. (for background)
Green opalescent, 1/2 sq. ft.
Red opalescent, 2 sq. in.
Blue opalescent, 2 sq. in.
Black, 1 sq. in.

Metals:
Black-backed copper foil tape, 3/16"
12 gauge copper wire (for hanging loops)
32" ladder chain

Tools & Other Supplies:
Jewelry glue
Basic Tools & Supplies for Copper Foil Method
Optional: Black patina

Step-by-Step

Prepare, Cut & Assemble:
1. Enlarge pattern to desired size and make an extra copy. Number and color-code each piece. Using pattern shears, cut out one copy of the pattern.
2. Adhere cutout pattern pieces to the glass. Cut out glass pieces.
3. On your work board, Tape or pin down the other copy of the pattern. Lay out and fit glass pieces to the pattern. Use your glass grinder to make any adjustments.

Apply Foil & Solder:
1. Wrap each piece of glass in 3/16" foil.
2. Solder all the pieces together, building up a nice smooth bead along the solder seams. Keep the solder joints low around the outside edges of the panel so the ladder chain will fit easily around the glass.
3. Turn over the project and solder the back the same as the front.

Finish:
1. Wrap the ladder chain around the outside edge of the panel. Secure the chain to the panel by soldering where the two ends meet.
2. Turn over the panel and solder the chain on the other side.
3. Using round nose pliers, make two loops of copper wire. Solder at the seams as shown on the pattern.
4. Clean up with soap and water.
5. Glue a drop of solder for the eye as indicated on the pattern. Let dry.
6. *Option:* Apply patina according to manufacturer's instructions. ✿

Enlarge to 120% for actual size

Enlarge to 254% for actual size

Instructions are on page 66

Lilies Mirror

Mirror, mirror on the wall, you're my favorite project of all. That's how I feel about this graceful mirror design. It's a great gift for someone really special.

Try a mix of great opalescent glass colors to create the floating glass frame. Copper wire used for the stamen adds a three-dimensional touch.

Size: 12" x 22"
Pattern on page 65

Supplies

Glass:
Green opalescent, various shades,
    1-1/2 sq ft.
Pink opalescent, various shades,
    1-1/2 sq. ft.
Mirror, 9" x 15"

Metals:
Copper foil tape, 7/32"
12 gauge copper wire (for hanging loops
    and stamen)

Tools & Other Supplies:
Basic Tools & Supplies for Copper Foil
    Method
Optional: Black patina

Step-by-Step

Prepare, Cut & Assemble:
1. Enlarge pattern to desired size and make an extra copy. Number and color-code each piece. Using pattern shears, cut out one copy of the pattern.
2. Adhere the cutout pattern pieces to the glass. Cut out glass pieces.
3. On your work board, pin or tape the other copy of the pattern.
4. Lay out and fit glass pieces to the pattern. Use your glass grinder to make any adjustments.
5. Cut the mirror to the shape of the dotted line on the pattern.

Apply Foil & Solder:
1. Wrap each piece of stained glass in 7/32" foil.
2. On the front, solder all the pieces together, building up a nice smooth bead along the solder seams. Turn over the project.
3. Wrap the edges of the mirror in foil and position it, right side down, on the stained glass frame. Solder the mirror to the frame.
4. Solder the back side of the stained glass frame the same as the front.

Finish:
1. Form the stamen with the copper wire. Puddle solder to create a drop of solder in the wire loops at ends of stamen. Solder stamen in place.
2. Clean up with soap and water.
3. *Option:* Apply patina according to manufacturer's instructions. ❋

Fuchsias Sconce

This colorful stained glass sconce is the perfect answer for adding color and style to larger spaces—at the corner of a sliding glass door, picture window, or window wall. It also can be used as a room divider (such as between a living room and a dining room). It's easy to install—simply screw the panel in place.

I used drapery glass for some of the flowers.
If you plan to use drapery glass, it is best cut with a glass saw.

Size: 31" x 32"

Supplies

Glass:
A wide variety of green and pink glasses (for the flowers and leaves)
Clear glass and white confetti glass (for the background)

Metals:
Black-backed copper foil tape, 3/16"
Black-backed copper foil tape, 7/32" or wider, depending on thickness of drapery glass (if using drapery glass)
1 6-ft. strip of 3/4" U zinc came
2 6-ft. strips of 1/4" U lead came
2 eye hooks, 1/2"

Tools & Other Supplies:
Basic Tools & Supplies for Copper Foil Method
Came saw *or* hacksaw
Optional: Black patina
Glass saw (recommended if working with drapery glass)

Step-by-Step

Prepare, Cut & Assemble:
1. Enlarge the pattern and make an extra copy.
2. Using pattern shears, cut out one copy of the pattern.
3. Adhere pattern pieces to the glass. Cut out each piece.
4. On your work board, tape or pin down the other copy of the pattern. Lay out and fit glass pieces to the pattern. Use your glass grinder to make any adjustments.
5. Using a came saw or hacksaw, cut zinc came to size.

Apply Foil & Solder:
1. Apply 3/16" foil tape to all the pieces except the drapery glass. Use 7/32" (or wider) foil for pieces cut from drapery glass.
2. Solder all the pieces together, building up a nice smooth bead along the solder seams. Keep the solder joints low around the outside edges of the sconce so the zinc and lead cames will fit easily on the edges.
3. Turn over the project and solder the back.

Finish:
1. Insert the eye hooks into the outside channel of the zinc framing. Solder firmly in place.
2. Slip the zinc came on the two straight sides of the sconce and hold in place with push pins or horseshoe nails. Make sure the zinc forms a true right angle. This is the corner you will attach to the window frame, wall, or ceiling.
3. Secure the zinc came to the panel by soldering at each foil/came intersection. Keep your solder joints small and neat.
4. Turn over the panel and solder the intersections on the back.
5. Stretch the lead came (see instructions on page 89). With the panel laying flat on the work table, wrap the lead came around the irregular edge of the sconce, securing with pushpins as you go.
6. Solder the lead came and foil where they intersect. Turn over the panel and solder the intersections on the back.

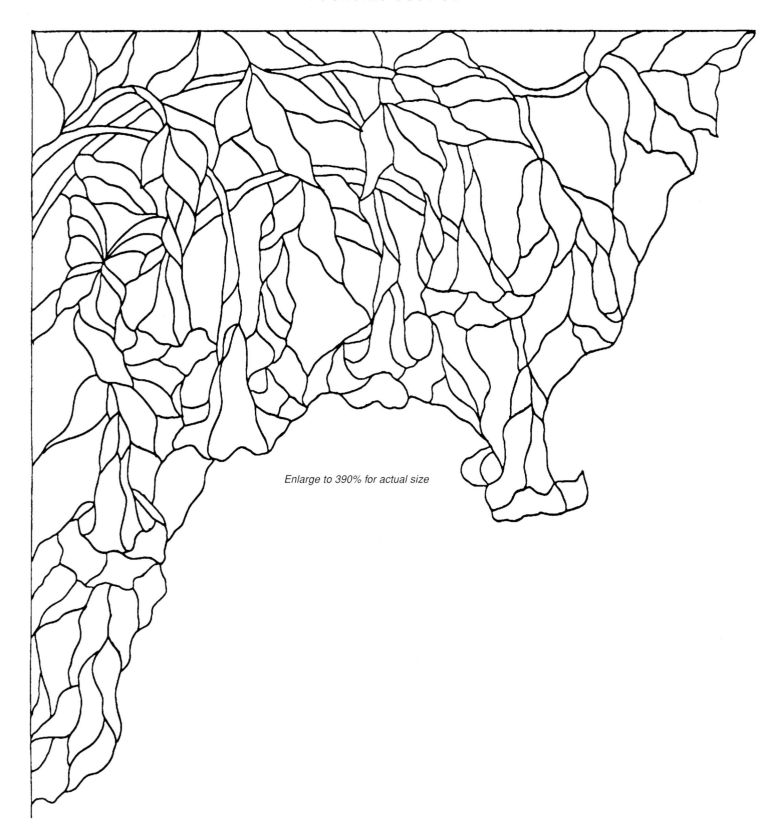

Enlarge to 390% for actual size

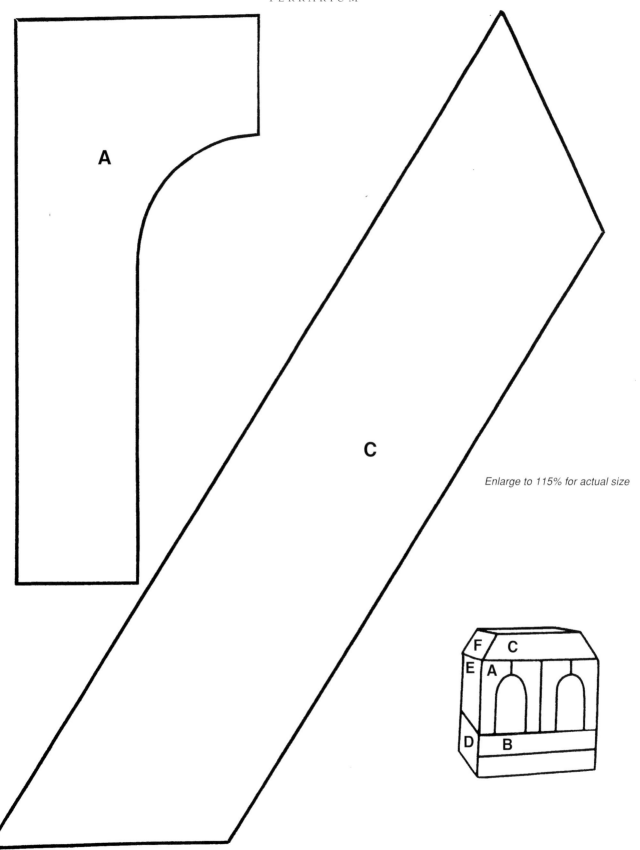

A

C

Enlarge to 115% for actual size

Terrarium

Size: 8" x 12" x 13-1/2" tall
Patterns on page 71

Supplies

Glass:
Clear seeded glass, 6 sq. ft.

Metals:
Black-backed copper foil tape, 7/32"

Tools & Other Supplies:
Basic Tools & Supplies for Copper Foil
    Method
Clear silicone caulk
Black patina

Step-by-Step

Prepare & Cut:
1. Enlarge pattern and make a copy.
2. Cut out one copy of the pattern.
3. Adhere the pattern pieces to the glass. Cut out the pieces as indicated:
   Piece A = 4 right and 4 left (from pattern)
   Piece B = 4 strips, each 2" x 12"
   Piece C = 2 (from pattern)
   Piece D = 2 strips, each 4" x 8"
   Piece E = 2 strips, each 7" x 8"
   Piece F = 2 strips, each 3" x 8"
   Piece G = 8" x 12" (the bottom)
4. On your work board, tape or pin the second copy of the pattern. Working panel by panel, lay out and fit glass pieces to the pattern. Use your glass grinder to make any adjustments.

Apply Foil & Solder:
1. Wrap each piece of glass with 7/32" foil.
2. Lay out the front panel and solder all the pieces together, building up a nice smooth bead over the front side of the panel. Turn over the panel and solder the back side.
3. Lay out the back panel and solder all the pieces together, building up a nice smooth bead over the front side of the panel. Turn over the panel and solder the back side.
4. To make the side panels, solder pieces D and E together. (Piece F will be added later.)
5. Lay out the four panels on your work table in this order, left to right: front, side, back, side with right sides facing up.
6. Use masking tape to join and hold the panels in place. With the taped sides facing out, lift panels up and form a rectangle, securing with additional tape as needed. *See Figs. 1 and 2.*
7. Square up the terrarium and tack solder the corners to secure shape.
8. Add the F pieces to the sides. Place piece G inside the bottom. Tack solder in place.
9. Solder all inside seams. Remove the tape.
10. Solder the outside seams. Build up a nice smooth bead over all inside and outside seams and edges.

Finish:
1. Clean up with soap and water.
2. Apply patina according to manufacturer's instructions.
3. Seal the seams inside the terrarium with clear silicone caulk to prevent water leakage. ✼

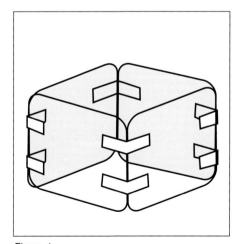

Figure 1

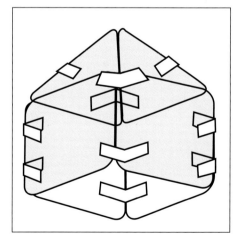

Figure 2

General Instructions for Making Boxes

Stained glass boxes make great gifts and are the perfect accessory for any tabletop. Once you learn this simple box-making technique, you can create all types and sizes of boxes and turn out dozens of gifts for your friends and family. You will not need a pattern unless you want to make a box with a decorative multi-piece top.

This cutting layout (Fig. 1) allows the grain of the glass to flow uninterrupted up the front of the box, across the top, and down the back. If the layout looks strange, just wait—as you assemble the box it will all come together and you will be delighted with the results.

Legend

SBT — Side B Top
SBB — Side B Bottom
SAT — Side A Top
SAB — Side A Bottom
BB — Back Bottom
BT — Back Top
T — Top
B — Bottom
FT — Front Top
FB — Front Bottom

Cut on solid lilnes first, then separate pieces as shown by dotted lines.

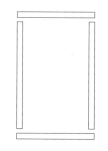

The box bottom is often cut from a different piece of glass.

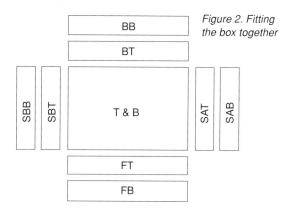

Figure 2. Fitting the box together

Fig. 3 - Placing pieces together (bird's-eye view) Long (front and back) sides are placed inside short sides.

Cutting & Assembling a Box

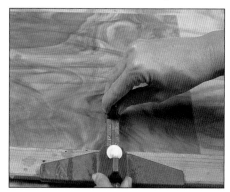

1. Use a strip cutter to cut the pieces of the box. If you have not worked with a strip cutter before, practice on scrap clear glass before you attempt to cut your art glass.

2. Wrap each piece with copper foil. Assemble and solder the top. Assemble the side pieces and solder at the corners to stabilize.

3. Box pieces are ready for final assembly

White Wave Box

This simple box top features wavy foil and some easy stippled soldering techniques.

Size: 6-1/4" x 4-1/4" x 2"

Supplies

Glass:
White opalescent glass, 14" x 6"
Mirror, for bottom, 1/8" thick, 4" x 6"

Metals:
Copper foil tape, 7/32"
"New Wave" foil tape, 7/32"
7" box chain
1 pair box hinges

Tools & Other Supplies:
Basic Tools & Supplies for Copper Foil
    Method
Needlenose pliers
Glass Strip Cutter

Step-by-Step

Cut & Assemble:

See "General Instructions for Making Boxes" before you start to cut.

1. Square up the white glass so all four corners are 90-degree angles. Make sure the edges are smooth and straight.
2. Mark the grain of the glass with a felt-tip marker.
3. Set your strip cutter for 2" strips. Cut one 2" x 6" strip of glass for the front of the box. Cut one 4" x 6" strip for the top. Reset your strip cutter and cut three 2" x 6" strips for the back and sides.
4. To make the shorter sides of the box, cut the side pieces to 4-1/4" long.
5. Separate the front, back and sides.
6. Lay out the cut pieces of glass as shown in the General Instructions. Smooth the edges and make adjustments.

Apply Foil & Solder:

1. Wrap the top piece with "New Wave" foil. Wrap the remaining pieces with 7/32" copper foil.
2. Following the General Instructions, assemble the side top pieces and side bottom pieces of the box and tack-solder.
3. Run a smooth solder bead over all inside copper seams. You do not need to solder the outside edges. Turn the lid over and solder the back.
4. To assemble the bottom of the box, wrap the mirror piece in foil and place flat on the work surface, mirror side up. Place the bottom side section around the mirror. Tack-solder the corners of the mirror to the corners of the box. Turn the box over and run a flat, smooth solder seam around the bottom edges, then solder the seams inside the box bottom.

Add Hinges:

Make hinges the same way as instructed for the Christmas Tree Box on page 77.

Finish:

1. Solder the front and back outside seams of the box. To stipple the solder, *gently* strike the solder line with the corner tip of the heated soldering iron. The heat from the iron will produce a small "hole". Randomly strike along the length of the solder line, being careful not to overheat a given section. If this occurs, simply smooth out the entire solder line, allow to cool and start again.
2. Solder a length of box chain inside the box to keep the lid from falling backward when opened.
3. Clean the project with soap and water. ✳

Christmas Tree Box

Christmas boxes are wonderful memory builders. This one features a simple landscape design illustrated with bright opalescent glass in holiday colors. In our family, we love getting out our decorations every holiday season and being reminded of memories they invoke.

Size: 6-1/4" x 4-1/4" x 2"

Supplies

Glass:
Red opalescent, for sides and top, 14" x 6"

Green opalescent, for tree on top, 4" square piece

White opalescent, for snow on top, 6" square piece

Green mirror, for bottom, 1/8" thick, 4" x 6"

Metals:
Copper foil tape, 7/32"
6" box chain
1 pair box hinges

Tools & Other Supplies:
Black patina
Basic Tools & Supplies for Copper Foil Method
Glass strip cutter
Needlenose pliers

Step-by-Step

Cut the Box Sides:
See "General Instructions for Making Boxes" before you start to cut.

1. Square up the red piece of glass so all four corners are 90-degree angles. Make sure the edges are smooth and straight.
2. Mark the grain of the glass with a felt-tip marker.
3. Set your strip cutter for 2" strips. Cut one 2" x 6" strip of glass for the front of the box. Cut three 2" x 6" strips for the back and sides.
4. To make the shorter sides of the box, cut the side pieces (pieces labeled SA and SB in the General Instructions) to 4-1/4" long. You can use the strip cutter or cut them by hand.
5. Now you are ready to separate the four box side bottoms (pieces labeled FB, BB, SAB, and SBB in the General Instructions) from the box side tops (pieces labeled FT, BT, SAT, and SBT). Set your strip cutter for 1". Follow the layout and double check the grain markings on the glass before you cut.

Make the Top:
1. Make two copies of the pattern.
2. Using pattern shears, cut out one copy of the pattern.
3. Adhere pattern pieces to the glass. Cut out each piece.

4. On your work board, tape or pin down the other copy of the pattern. Lay out and fit glass pieces to the pattern. Use your glass grinder to make any adjustments.

Assemble:

Lay out the cut pieces of glass as shown in the General Instructions. Use a grinder to smooth the edges of the cut pieces and make adjustments. The edges of each glass piece must be smooth and straight.

Apply Foil & Solder:

1. Wrap all the pieces with 7/32" copper foil.
2. Following the General Instructions, assemble the side top pieces and side bottom pieces of the box and tack-solder. Make sure the top fits easily inside the top sides.
3. Run a smooth solder bead over all inside copper seams. You do not need to solder the outside edges. Turn the lid over and solder the back.
4. To assemble the bottom of the box, wrap the mirror piece in foil and place flat on the work surface, mirror side up. Place the bottom side section around the mirror. The mirror should fit easily into the box. Tack-solder the corners of the mirror to the corners of the box. Turn the box over and run a flat, smooth solder seam around the bottom edges, then solder the seams inside the box bottom.

Add Hinges:

1. Fit the top and bottom of the box together. Make sure you are happy with the fit. Secure with two rubber bands to help hold them together while you solder the hinges.
2. Position the hinges on the back of the box. Hold the hinges in place with needlenose pliers. Using a cotton swab or small paintbrush, paint flux on the edge of the hinge. *Tip:* Don't use too much flux or the solder will run into your hinge and ruin it. Remember solder can't travel where there is no flux.

Finish:

1. Solder the front and back outside seams of the box.
2. Solder a length of box chain inside the box to keep the lid from falling backward when opened.
3. Clean the project with soap and water.
4. Apply black patina according to package instructions. ❁

Pattern is actual size

Drapery Glass Box

Drapery glass was first developed by the Tiffany Studios to replace the heavy painting that earlier artists used to decorate the folds in the robes of biblical characters in church windows. It is still being made by some of today's better glass factories. The beauty of this glass is all you need to inspire a box project. The drapery glass is used on the top of this one.

Size: 6" x 4-1/2" x 2"

Supplies

Glass:
Champagne drapery glass, for top,
    4-1/2" x 6"
Champagne opalescent glass, for front,
    back, and sides, 8" x 6"
Mirror, for bottom, 1/8" thick, 4-1/2" x 6"

Metals:
Copper foil tape, 7/32"
7" box chain
1 pair box hinges

Tools & Other Supplies:
Optional: Copper patina
Basic Tools & Supplies for Copper Foil
    Method
Needlenose pliers
Strip cutter

Step-by-Step

Cut & Assemble:
*See "General Instructions for Making Boxes"
    before you start to cut.*

1. Square up the pieces of glass so all four corners of all pieces are 90-degree angles.
2. Mark the grain of the glass with a felt-tip marker.
3. Set your strip cutter for 2" strips. Cut four 2" x 6" strips of glass for the front, back and sides.
4. To make the shorter sides of the box, cut the side pieces to 4-1/2" long.

5. Separate the four front, back and side pieces. Set your strip cutter for 1".
6. Lay out the cut pieces of glass as shown in the General Instructions.

Apply Foil & Solder:
1. Wrap all the pieces with 7/32" copper foil.
2. Following the General Instructions, assemble the side top pieces and side bottom pieces.
3. Run a smooth solder bead over all inside copper seams. You do not need to solder the outside edges. Turn the lid over and solder the back.
4. To assemble the bottom of the box, wrap the mirror piece in foil and place flat on the work surface, mirror side up. Place the bottom side section around the mirror. Tack-solder the corners of the mirror to the corners of the box. Turn the box over and run a flat, smooth solder seam around the bottom edges, then solder the seams inside the box bottom.

Add Hinges:
Follow hinge instructions for Christmas Tree Box on page 77.

Finish:
Follow finish instructions for Christmas Tree Box on page 77. ✸

Beveled Box

I took a glass beveling course in Detroit 25 years ago; my instructor was pretty good. For our "graduation piece," we had to cut a 1/4" plate glass rectangle in half using a gentle curve, and then we had to bevel it! Hours later, I knew two things—one, I would starve as a custom beveler and two, I wanted to make something using my first real bevel. So I made a box for the only person that could ever really appreciate all my hard homework—my mom.

Size: 6-1/4" x 4-1/4" x 2"

Supplies

Glass:
2 beveled glass pieces that, placed end to end, measure 4" x 6" (for top)
Purple cathedral glass, 14" x 6"
Mirror, 1/8" thick, 4" x 6" (for bottom)

Metals:
Copper foil tape, 7/32"
7" box chain
1 pair box hinges

Tools & Other Supplies:
Basic Tools & Supplies for Copper Foil Method
Glass strip cutter
Needlenose pliers

Step-by-Step

Cut & Assemble:
See "General Instructions for Making Boxes" before you start to cut.

1. Square up the purple cathedral glass so all four corners are 90-degree angles.
2. Mark the grain of the glass with a felt-tip marker.
3. Set your strip cutter for 2" strips. Cut four 2" x 6" strips of glass for the front, back, and sides.
4. To make the shorter sides of the box, cut the side pieces to 4-1/4" long.
5. Now you are ready to separate the four box side bottoms from the box side tops. Set your strip cutter for 1".
6. Lay out the cut pieces of glass as shown in the General Instructions.

Apply Foil & Solder:
1. Wrap all the pieces with 7/32" copper foil.
2. Following the General Instructions, assemble the side top pieces and side bottom pieces.
3. Run a smooth solder bead over all inside copper seams. You do not need to solder the outside edges. Turn the lid over and solder the back.
4. To assemble the bottom of the box, wrap the mirror piece in foil and place flat on the work surface, mirror side up. Place the bottom side section around the mirror. Tack-solder the corners of the mirror to the corners of the box. Turn the box over and run a flat, smooth solder seam around the bottom edges, then solder the seams inside the box bottom.

Add Hinges:
Follow hinge instructions for Christmas Tree Box on page 77.

Finish:
Follow finish instructions for Christmas Tree Box on page 77. ❈

Lead Came Method

The lead came method is the more traditional technique of crafting stained glass. Pieces of glass are cut and fit into metal channels called cames. Came comes in a variety of sizes and metal types; the most common is lead, but you will also find came made from hard metals such as zinc, brass, and copper. The places where cames meet or intersect within a project are called joints. The joints are soldered to create a strong, continuous metal frame around each individual glass piece within the project.

Leaded stained glass is a beautiful puzzle that's easy to construct one step at a time—a piece of lead, a piece of glass, a piece of lead, a piece of glass until the panel is completed. In this section, you'll see how to cut out a pattern, cut glass, use a grinder, lead up the panel, solder, and frame the finished project for display.

The projects in this section include a variety of panels, a mirror, and a lampshade. Each project includes one or more photographs, a list of supplies you'll need, and step-by-step instructions for cutting, assembling, and finishing. Before you start any project in this section, review the instructions and the photographs in the Crafting with Lead Came section.

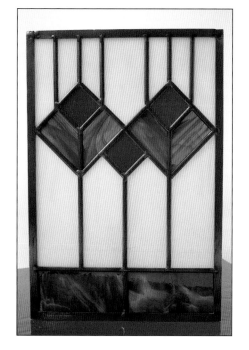
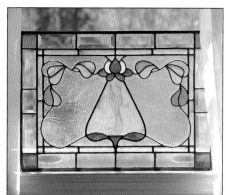

Basic Supplies for the Lead Came Method

The following supplies are a check list of items you will need for creating projects using this crafting method. These supplies and tools have been pictured and explained in the chapter entitled "Supplies for Getting Started."

Pattern Making Supplies:

- Pattern fixative or rubber cement
- Pencil and eraser
- Felt-tip pen or china marker
- Pattern paper
- 18" metal ruler with cork back
- Transfer and tracing paper
- Colored pencils
- Pattern shears

Glass Cutting & Breaking Tools:

- Glass cutter
- Lubricating oil
- Carborundum stone or emery cloth
  Optional: Grinder
- Breaking pliers
- Running pliers
- Grozing pliers
  Optional: Combination Pliers

Assembly Supplies:

- Work board
- Glass Squaring bars
- Desk brush and dust pan for cleanup
- Masking tape
- Cloth for wiping edges
- Lead spacers which are small pieces of scrap came

Soldering Supplies:

- Solder
- Soldering iron with 1/4" tip
- Rheostat
- Soldering iron stand
- Tip cleaner
- Flux and flux brush

Safety gear:

- Safety glasses
- Face mask

Additional Supplies

Here are some specific supplies used only for this crafting method.
These are in addition to all the "Basic Supplies" listed.

Came

The leaded glass technique connects individual pieces of glass by fitting them into metal channels called cames. Came comes in a variety of sizes and metal types; the most common is lead, but you will also find came made from hard metals such as zinc, brass, and copper. The places cames meet or intersect within a project are called joints. The joints are soldered to create a strong, continuous metal frame around each individual glass piece within the project.

There are two basic came shapes. **H-shaped cames** are used in the interior portions of a project because they are designed to accept glass from two sides. **U-shaped cames** are used to wrap the exterior perimeter of a panel or an individual piece of glass when constructing of a box, candle cube, or birdhouse.

Came is sold in 6-foot strips of various sizes. The size is determined by the width of the came face. The face can be flat, round, or colonial. The channel height is generally 3/16" high, but you can special order what are called "high heart" cames, which have a bigger channel, for projects such as pressing flowers between two pieces of glass.

Select your came size based on the size of the glass pieces and the intricacy of the design. The smaller the came face, the less support it provides large glass pieces; the larger the face, the bulkier the look. If you are building a front door panel with bevels, you would want 3/8" or 3/16" came. But for a floral window with lots of small pieces, you would use 1/16" or 1/8" came. Lead, unlike foil, gives you a smooth flowing lead line that highlights the design, not the metal.

Choosing Came

The decision to work with lead came or one of the hard metal came types depends on the size of the project, where the project will be installed, and how many curves are in the design. Lead is very flexible, easy to work with, and can easily be cut and trimmed to shape using lead nippers or a lead knife.

Hard metal cames extruded from brass, zinc, or copper provide maximum strength but can be more difficult to work with, especially if your project contains curved lines and angles. Some gentle shapes and curves can be done by hand, but others re-

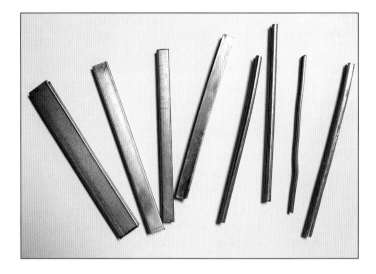

quire the use of a came bender. Hard metal cames must be cut with a hacksaw or power came saw. If you are going to work with hard metal came, do yourself the favor of investing in a good came saw and a came bender. They will provide you years of unlimited design and project possibilities.

Cames are also selected because of their colors. Brass cames are elegant, and brass provides excellent strength and lasting beauty. Zinc cames are silver, and they work very well in contemporary panels or when sparkle of both glass and metals is desired. Copper came is perfect for southwestern-style panels or when matching copper or Arts & Crafts hardware or decor. All solder joints are silver but can be treated with a patina or painted to match any color of came.

Whether you work with lead or hard metal came, the process of assembling your panel or project is called "leading up."

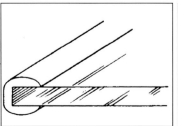

U-Shaped Came.

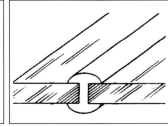

H-Shaped Came.

Leading Knife

A leading knife primarily is used to cut lead cames into various lengths. The blade needs to be sharpened regularly to keep from crushing the heart of the came when cutting. The end of the handle has a lead inlay, which is used to gently tap glass pieces into the came channels or to hammer horseshoe nails into your work board when leading up a project.

Lead Nippers

A quick and easy way to trim lead came is with nippers. Nippers are best for cutting straight cuts or slight angles. For more long, tapered cuts, a lead knife works best. You will want to learn how to use both tools.

Came Saw

A came saw is a small power chop saw that uses a fiber or metal circular blade to cut hard metal cames. It is a must if you are going to build one or more large panels with hard metal came.

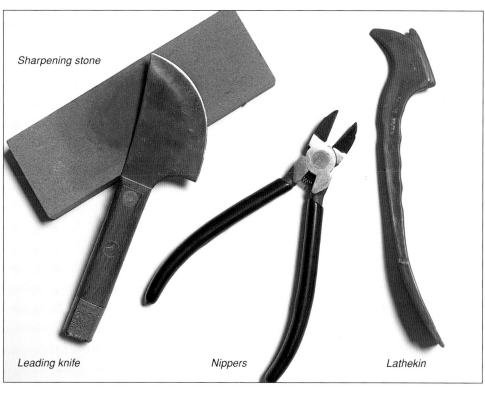

Sharpening stone

Leading knife   Nippers   Lathekin

Came Bender

Hard metal cames benefit greatly from being bent with a came bender. The device bends the came without scarring the came face or crushing the channel. The bender's rotating wheels can be adjusted to conform to almost any shape. Came benders can be permanently attached to your work table or held securely (but temporarily) with a c-clamp.

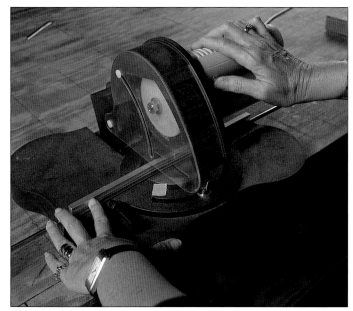

A came saw is used to cut hard metal came.

Lathekin (Fid)

Opening crushed or tight came channels is easier with a lathekin, which is also called a fid.

Lead Vise

All lead cames must be stretched before you use them. Stretching takes out any small kinks and adds strength. A lead vise holds one end of the came while you hold the opposite end with a pair of **household pliers** and gently pull or stretch the came.

Came Notcher

A came notcher is used to cut 1/8" U-shaped hard metal came at a 45-degree angle without cutting through the back spine of the came, giving you perfectly mitered corners for framing projects or wrapping individual glass pieces.

If you do not have a notcher, you can cut U-shaped cames with wire cutters or nippers.

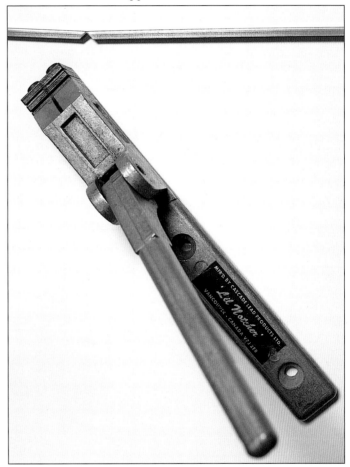

Horseshoe Nails

Horseshoe nails have two flat sides and a large square head. They are used to hold pieces of glass in the channels while the panel is being leaded up. They hammer into a wooden work board easily and can be pulled free with just a gentle wiggle. Horseshoe nails bend easy. When they do, throw them away. Trying to work with a bent nail isn't worth the hassle.

Crafting with Lead Came

In this section, you'll see how to cut out a pattern, cut glass, prepare and cut lead came, assemble and solder, and add the finishing touches to a project.

Step 1 • Prepare Your Pattern

When creating a pattern for a lead came project you must take into consideration the space taken up by the lead heart and outside edges of the came.

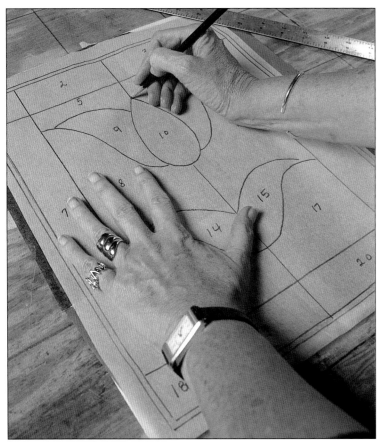

2. Use arrows to mark the desired direction of the grain of the glass on your two working copies of the pattern (the one you will cut apart and the one you will use for assembling). Number the pattern pieces. *Option:* Color-code the pattern with colored pencils that correspond with glass colors you've chosen. This makes it easier to identify the pattern pieces after you've cut them apart for the cutting templates.

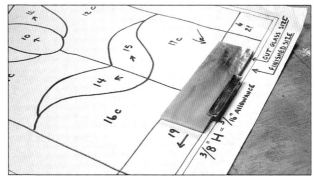

1. Position tracing paper over the pattern and trace the design lines with a pencil. Transfer the design using transfer paper to white pattern paper or photocopy the traced design and enlarge as noted. You want to have two copies of the pattern—one to cut apart to make templates for cutting the glass and another to use as a guide when assembling the piece.

3. The two patterns are ready to have their edges trimmed. The "finished size" is the size your project will be once it is completed. The "cut size" is the size you will cut your glass pieces; the cut size dimensions take into account the came heart and outside channel of the lead (and so end up the "finished size"). The "sight size" of a piece is the area you actually see after the glass is inserted in the came channel.

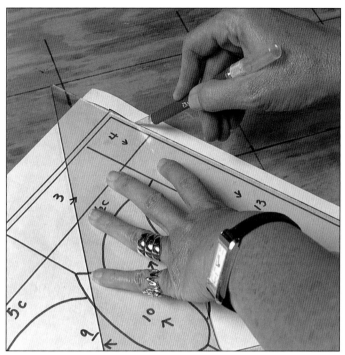

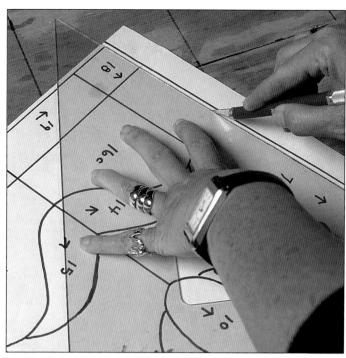

4. Using a craft knife, cut out the pattern for assembling the piece on the "finished size" lines. Use a ruler or a triangle to get a clean, straight edge.

5. Use the second traced pattern for making templates. Cut out the outer edges of the pattern you will be using for cutting the glass pieces on the "cut size" lines, using a ruler or triangle and a craft knife to get a clean, straight edge.

6. Use pattern shears to cut out the pattern pieces you will use as cutting templates. Put the single blade up toward you and start cutting with small strokes, not big sweeping ones. Hold the pattern in your other hand and cut right along the line, cutting in the crux of the shears. The three blades of the pattern shears work together to remove a strip of paper that accommodates the space needed for the came heart. Continue cutting until you have cut out every piece of your pattern. The order you cut it out in doesn't matter; do whatever seems easiest for you.

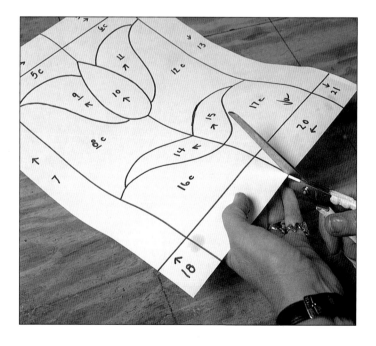

Step 2 • Cut the Glass Pieces

Caution! Always wear safety glasses to protect your eyes when cutting glass.

1. Determine how much glass you will need to cut your first piece by positioning the pattern piece on the glass. Score a smaller piece of glass from the larger piece, using your glass cutter. (You'll cut out the pattern piece—in this case, it's a leaf—from the smaller piece of glass.) Begin scoring, positioning your glass cutter at the edge of the large piece. Pull the wheel of the cutter down the length of the glass to make a score.

To break the glass, pick it up and put your fingers on each side of the scored line, under the glass with your thumbs on top. Rock your hands up and away from you. The glass will break along the scored line.

2. Apply pattern fixative or rubber cement to the backs of the pattern pieces. There is a right side and a wrong side to glass for cutting. The right side—the front—is generally smoother. The wrong side—the back—has a little bit of a bump to it. Position the pattern pieces on the right (smooth) side of glass, aligning the arrows you marked on the pattern pieces with the grain of the glass. Allow 1/4-1/2" all around each piece to make breaking out the pieces easier.

Cut the larger piece into two smaller pieces, scoring a line between the pattern pieces. Break the glass.
Option: If you have a light box, you can place the pattern on the light box and position the glass over the pattern. (The pattern lines will be visible through the glass.) Use a china marker or felt-tip marker (one that's not permanent on glass) to transfer the pattern lines to the glass.

3. To begin cutting the first pattern piece, start the cut at the edge of the piece of glass and move the cutter to the edge of the pattern template. Finish the cut by continuing past the edge of the pattern template and off the edge of the glass. This photo shows scoring the inside curve.

4. Break the glass with breaking pliers. Hold the glass off the work surface in one hand and hold the pliers in your other hand. Position the edge of the pliers on the scored line. Breaking pliers work well on curved cuts. Use the same technique to score and break the outside curve.

5. Use grozing pliers to break away any small chips or flanges of glass that protrude on the edges of cut pieces. You will save a lot of time if you use your grozing pliers to remove most of the unwanted glass before you use the grinder or smoothing stone. **TIP:** To ensure a clean work surface, periodically sweep off your work surface with a brush to remove small chips and slivers of glass that accumulate as you work.

6. Smooth the edges of each cut piece with a carborundum stone or a piece of emery cloth. Or use an electric grinder to smooth the edges. Keep the pattern pieces attached to the glass as you work on the edges.

7. To cut deep curves, make successive scores and breaks to gradually move into the final cut. The dotted lines show how this background piece could be scored and separated.

8. Use running pliers on straight cuts, like this border piece. Score the glass from one edge to the other along the pattern template's edge. Align the mark on the running pliers with the scored line. Squeeze the pliers to break the glass.

Step 3 • Preparing & Cutting Lead Came

1. Lead cames must be stretched before you use them. **Never** stretch came until you are ready to lead up your panel—and then **only** stretch the came you will be using that day. Once came is stretched, it starts to oxidize. The oxidation process tarnishes the came and makes it more difficult to solder if left for a period of time.

To estimate how much you will need, use a tape measure to measure the leading lines in your pattern. Add the measurements together and add 25% of that number to the total.

The first step in stretching the came is to insert one end of the piece in a lead vise. To stretch, hold the other end of the came with a pair of pliers and pull. The stretching process requires a little experience to know when you have stretched the lead just the right amount. Generally speaking, you want to stretch a 6-ft. piece of came 3-4". Overstretching the came will stress the lead, making it stiffer, and will narrow the channel height, making it more difficult to insert glass in the channel. Once your came is stretched, remove it from the vise. Use your lead nippers to trim 2" off each end of the came, and discard the lead scraps.

2. Using your lead nippers, cut six to ten 2" strips of came to be used as spacers while leading up the panel. If you are working with two or more sizes of came, cut additional spacers from each size. Have lots of horseshoe nails on hand and a pointed felt-tip marker.

3. Draw a lathekin (fid) down the lead channel on one side; then turn the strip over and repeat on the other side. This removes dents (small or large) and opens up the channel so the glass will fit in it easily.

4. To cut came, place the came on a firm wooden surface, channel side up. Place a sharp leading knife blade on the lead. Gently push down with the knife while rocking it side to side until it cuts through the channel and heart.

The leading knife is a valuable tool that must be kept sharp for cutting to avoid crushing the came. To make sure your leading knife is nice and sharp, sharpen it regularly on a sharpening stone.

5. To cut angles with the knife, place the came channel side up and place the blade at a 45 degree angle. Use that same rocking motion to cut a longer miter.

Angles also can be cut with lead nippers. Mark the angle on the came; then use the nippers to make a straight cut first. Line up the nippers with the mark on the came and cut the angle.

Note: Don't bother saving leftover pieces of lead. Check with your local recycling facility or sanitation department about disposal of discarded lead scraps.

Step 4 • Assemble the Project

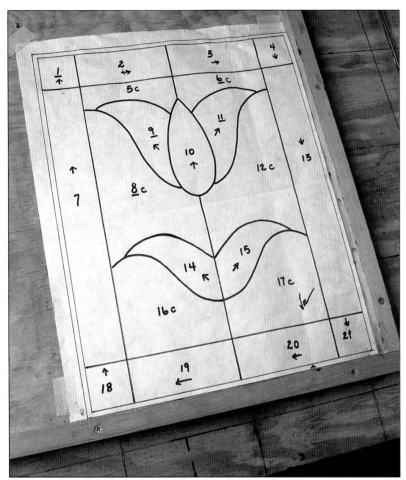

1. Use your second copy of the pattern as a guide for leading up your project. Start by using a craft knife and ruler to trim off two edges of the pattern at the "finished size" line to form a trimmed right angle that can be positioned in the corner of your work board. (You will learn with experience that it is often easier to lead up a panel if you start in one corner.) Use masking tape to secure your pattern to the work board.

Lay out all your glass pieces in numerical order or, if space allows, lay them out in the mirror image of the design. You will remove the pattern pieces from the glass as you use each piece but for now leave the patterns attached to the cut pieces.

2. Cut two pieces of perimeter came the same length as the panel you are building. Place them on top of your pattern alongside the wooden stop molding.

3. Secure the ends of the came pieces with horseshoe nails.

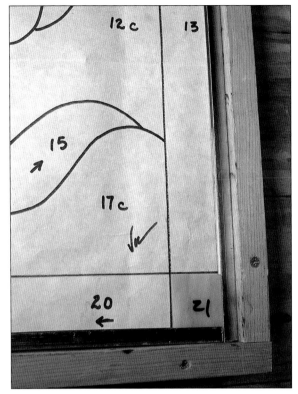

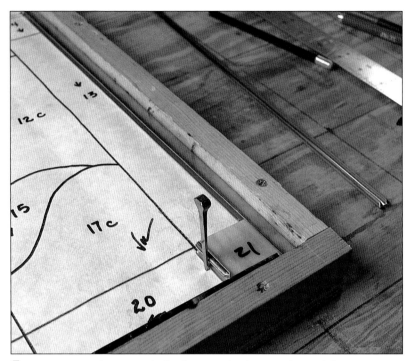

4. Matching the numbers on the pattern to the numbers on the glass pieces, select the first corner piece. Remove the pattern paper from the piece and slip the glass in the lead came channels. Check around the outside edges of the glass piece. Make sure you can see the pattern line around all the exposed edges. If not, mark the area on the glass with your felt-tip marker and remove the piece. Use the glass grinder or grozing pliers to remove the excess glass. Continue putting in and checking the piece until it fits perfectly!

The secret to successfully building lead came windows is to stay on pattern. If you're ever tempted to tell yourself "maybe this won't be a problem," resist! Stop, take out the piece, and fix it. This goes for a piece that's too small as well as for one that's too large. If there is too much space between the edge of the glass piece and the pattern line, the glass piece may not stay in the channel.

5. Once you are happy with the fit, use a lead spacer (one of the pieces you cut or a small discarded piece of came) to "face the glass"—simply slip the spacer on the outside edge of the glass piece and secure with a horseshoe nail. **Never** put a nail directly against the edge of the glass or a good piece of came (one you're using to build your project). The nail will chip the glass and mar the face of the came.

6. Fit a piece of lead came on the edge of the glass and mark for cutting. This photo shows marking the lead by denting it with a leading knife.

7. Using lead nippers, cut the marked piece of lead came to fit against the glass.

8. Place the lead against the glass piece.

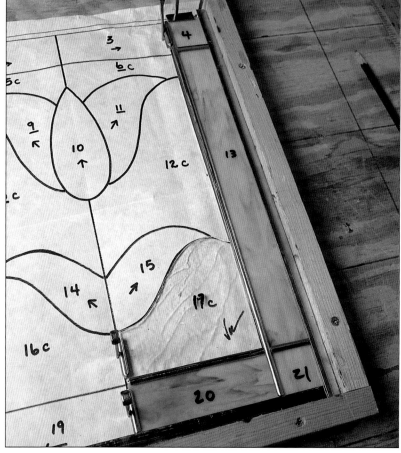

9. Continue to add pieces of glass and pieces of lead, working up the right side. Cut and fit a piece of lead along the left side of all three glass pieces. Add the piece of glass along the bottom, then the first interior piece.

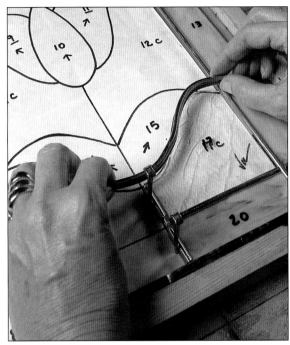

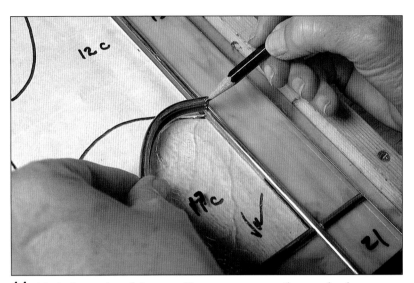

11. Mark the angles of the cuts. You can use a pencil to mark where to cut the lead or dent the lead with a knife to indicate the cutting line. This photo shows marking the lead with a pencil. Trim the lead to size.

10. Curved pieces are easy to lead up because lead came is very pliable. Cut off a section of came that's large enough to wrap along the outside edge of the glass piece. Position the came over the top of the glass edge and gently mold the came with your hands to mirror the angle of the glass piece.

12. Remove the nail and spacer and slip the trimmed came in place. Push the came up on the glass edge and continue to mold the lead to fit the glass. *Tip:* Use the end of your fid to get a nice snug fit. Secure this lead came in place using another lead spacer and a nail. This is called "facing the came."

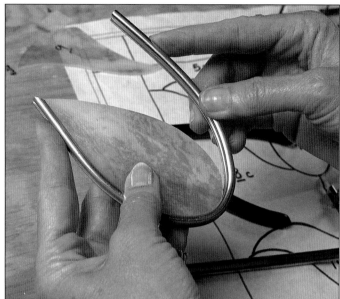

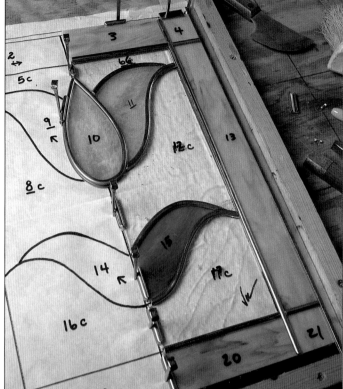

13. The center petal of the tulip is wrapped with a piece of came. First, cut a piece of came long enough to fit around the piece and cut a 45-degree angle on one end. *Tip:* It's better to have a piece of came that's a little too long. You can always trim off, but you can't add. Wrap the piece, making sure the glass is secure in the channel. Where the ends meet, mark the end and cut the came at an angle for a smooth fit.

14. Place center piece. This photos shows the right half of the panel leaded up.

15. Once all the pieces are leaded up, you are ready to finish your panel by adding the two remaining perimeter came pieces. This is called "capping off." Place the pieces of came on the top and left side. To make sure the edge pieces are secure, slip a squaring bar the length of the panel in the outside lead channel (or against the back of the lead, if the panel is framed in U-shaped came).

Check to make sure you can still see your "finished size" pattern line around the edges of the came. If not, use the lead inlay in the handle of your leading knife to gently tap along the edge of the squaring bars. This will evenly shift all the glass pieces at once and allow you to snug up your design and correct minor out-of-square problems.

Step 5 • Solder the Panel

To solder lead came, use 50/50 solder and a soldering iron-and-rheostat combination or a thermostatically controlled iron of 80 to 100 watts.

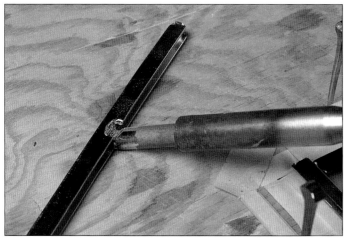

1. Test the temperature by holding the soldering iron tip on a scrap piece of lead came. If it melts the lead, it is too hot. Turn the iron down and re-test in a few minutes. You want your iron hot enough to quickly turn solder into a flowing liquid but not so hot that it melts the lead came.

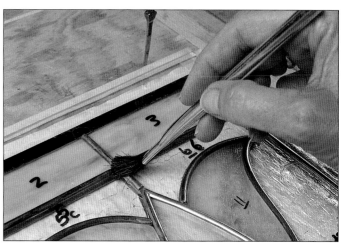

2. Paint the solder joints with flux to prepare them for solder. Don't worry about being exact with the flux.

3. Place the end of the solder wire over the joint and apply heat, using the flat side of the iron. Hold in place until the solder flows smooth and flat over the joint. Use just enough solder to hide the lead's intersection but not so much that there's a ridge or a "button."

Keep solder joints small and flat round the perimeter of the panel so it will be easier to frame or install. When you complete one side, turn over the panel and solder the other side.

Soldering Tips
- Always use a soldering iron stand to secure your iron.
- If you need to re-heat a solder joint to touch up or lower a tall solder joint, always re-flux first.
- Solder will not stick to glass, but avoid touching the tip of your hot soldering iron to the glass surface.

Soldering Hard Metals
Soldering hard metal came is a little different than soldering lead came. You can use more heat because the hard metals don't melt as quickly. Hard metals require less solder because they are not as porous. Because hard metals heat much more quickly than lead, **never** try to hold a piece of hard metal in place with your fingers while soldering.

Step 6 • Cementing

All came panels should be cemented. Cementing makes the panel airtight and waterproof and keeps the glass from rattling inside the came channels. You can mix up cement using my formula (the recipe follows) or use pre-mixed cement. (Pre-mixed leaded glass cement is not my first choice, but it works in a pinch and is handy when you need to touch up a panel after a repair.)

*Cementing is a messy process, best done outside or in your garage. Because you will be working with dusty powders, you **must** work in a well-ventilated area and wear a respirator or dust mask.*

Tools for Cementing

2 natural fiber nail brushes *or* 2 small scrub brushes
A mixing container
Stir stick
Wooden chopstick or dowel sharpened in a pencil sharpener
Respirator or dust mask

Formula Ingredients

4 parts whiting (chalk dust)
2 parts plaster of Paris
1-1/2 parts turpentine
1 part boiled linseed oil
1 part Portland cement
Optional: Powdered lamp black or grout colorant (to color)

Tools & Other Supplies

Additional whiting
Newspapers

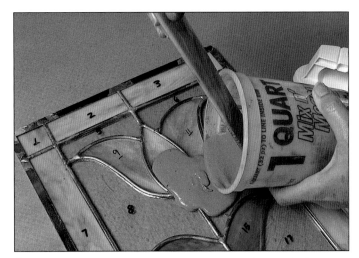

1. Cover your work table with newspapers or brown kraft paper. Make sure the surface is smooth and free of debris so you won't crack your glass while you work.

Mix your cement using the ingredients listed previously. Mix enough for about one pint of cement. Place ingredients in a container. *Option:* Sprinkle lamp black or colorant over the ingredients. Using the stir stick, mix to the consistency of mayonnaise. Add whiting to thicken; add turpentine to thin. *Or* purchase pre-mixed cement.

Place your panel on a covered work table and pour the cement mixture on the panel.

2. Work the mixture around the panel, using a brush in a circular motion. Be sure to push it under the face of the came, filling in any gaps or spaces around the glass and cames. Wipe off any excess cement with the edge of your cement brush.

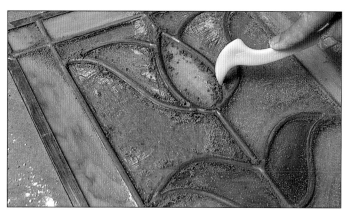

3. Sprinkle a light dusting of whiting over the panel. Using a clean brush, repeat the same circular motion. The whiting dries up excess moisture, helps clean the glass, and creates a natural patina from the lead came to color the solder joints. The more you work, the more beautiful your project will become. Sweep off the remaining whiting. Sprinkle with a second light dusting of whiting and brush again.

4. Use the fid, a chopstick or a sharpened wooden dowel to "dress the came" by removing excess cement from the panel. Try to create a clean edge around each piece of came.

Change the paper on your work table, turn over the panel, and repeat the entire process on the other side. When you have cemented both sides, allow the panel to lay flat on a clean, dry surface for at least 24 hours. (I like to allow at least 48 hours for the cement on a large panel to set and cure.)

When the cement is dry, it's time for the final cleanup. Clean your glass with whiting and a soft cloth and/or soap and water. Go easy with the water. A coffee filter makes an excellent drying cloth—it doesn't leave lint or fuzz behind.

Step 7 • Adding a Patina

Depending on the color of the came you are working with, you may wish to apply patina to the solder joints or use a paint pen to color the joints so they blend better with the color of the came metal. Patinas are specially formulated colorants for lead, zinc, and brass. They can change silver solder joints to varying shades of copper or make them black. Several brands of patinas are available at craft and metal stores.

Apply the patina to solder joints using a cotton swab. Don't dip directly into your patina; that weakens its strength. Pour a small amount into a small container or the cap of the patina container. Two or three coats may be necessary. Polish black patina with liquid auto wax. Buff copper with red jeweler's rouge, which is available at lapidary and jeweler's supply stores.

My Recipe for Copper Patina

For years I have used this recipe to make my own copper patina. After buffing with red jeweler's rouge, the metal will be a golden pink color.

4 oz. water

2 tablespoons copper sulfate (available at hardware stores)

1 tablespoon lemon juice (artificial works, too)

Rainbow Mirror Panel

Give the gift of rainbows and sunshine when you make this panel that includes a mirror.
Use a strip cutter for accurate, easy cutting of long, straight pieces.

Size: 10-5/8" x 19-1/4"
Pattern on page 102

Supplies

Glass:
Mirror, 8-1/8" x 11"
White opalescent glass
Pink and yellow opalescent glass
Yellow opalescent glass
Green opalescent glass
Red opalescent glass
Brown opalescent glass

Metals:
2 6-ft. strips of 1/8" H lead came
1 6-ft. strip of 1/8" U zinc came

Tools & Other Supplies:
Black patina
Basic Tools & Supplies for Lead Came
    Method
Cementing supplies
Option: Strip cutter

Step-by-Step

Prepare & Cut Glass:
1. Make two copies of the pattern. Number and mark the grain line on each piece. Using pattern shears, cut out the design from one copy.
2. Adhere pattern pieces to the glass and cut out each piece.
3. Use grozing pliers to remove any chips or protrusions on the glass pieces. Smooth the edges with a grinder or carborundum stone as needed to fit the pattern.

Lead Up & Solder:
1. On your work board, tape or pin the second copy of the pattern. Cut two 1/8" U came pieces and place along the top edge and one side edge of the work board.
2. Lead up the panel using 1/8" H came, working from one corner, placing a piece of lead, a piece of glass, and so on, until all pieces are in place. Use the grinder to smooth edges of the glass and make any necessary adjustments to keep your glass pieces within the pattern lines. Each piece must fit the pattern lines or your panel will be impossible to complete.
3. Cap off the project with the last two pieces of 1/8" U came.
4. Solder the lead joints on the front of the panel.
5. Turn over the panel and solder the back side.

Finish:
1. Protect the mirror by masking it off with newspaper. Cement the panel, following the instructions in the "Crafting with Lead Came" section.
2. Clean the panel. ❈

Arts & Crafts Lampshade

Lampshades are one of my favorite "glass rewards"—you don't honestly get to see the results of all your work until the shade is married with its hardware and someone flips the switch. I must say I have never been disappointed. Are there things I'd change? Always. This lampshade, designed in the Arts and Crafts style of the early 20th century, is a great project for launching your own lamp rewards.

Hard metal cames, like the brass used here, can be used to make lampshades. This shade takes its inspiration from the Arts & Crafts movement of the early 20th century.

Size: 7" x 11-1/2"
Pattern on page 103

Supplies

Glass:
Amber opalescent, 2-1/2 sq. ft. (for background)
Purple opalescent, 2-1/2" x 6" piece
Green opalescent, 6" x 6" piece

Metals:
1 6-ft. strip of 1/8" H brass came
2 6-ft. strips of 1/8" U brass came

Tools & Other Supplies:
Vase cap
Gold paint pen
Basic Tools & Supplies for Lead Came Method

Step-by-Step

Prepare & Cut Glass:
Use these instructions to make four identical panels.
1. Make two copies of the pattern. Number and mark the grain line on each piece. Using pattern shears, cut out design from one copy.
2. Adhere pattern pieces to the glass and cut out each piece.
3. Use grozing pliers to remove any chips or protrusions on the glass pieces. Smooth the edges with a grinder or carborundum stone as needed to fit the pattern.

Lead Up & Solder Panels:
Use these instructions to make four identical panels.
1. On your work board, tape or pin the second copy of the pattern.
2. Lead up the panel, working from one corner, placing a piece of brass came, a piece of glass, and so on, until all pieces are in place. Use the grinder to smooth edges of the glass and make any necessary adjustments to keep your glass pieces within the pattern lines. Each piece must fit the pattern lines or your

panel will be impossible to complete.
3. Cap off the project with the last two pieces of brass came.
4. Solder the joints on the front of the panel.
5. Turn over the panel and solder the back side.

Assembling the Lamp:
Build the lamp on a surface that will accept pushpins. I prefer Homasote but it can be difficult to find. An option is to use a ceiling tile.
1. Lay panels face down on work surface. Place ample masking tape to back of panels.
2. Heat soldering iron. Raise panels into the desired shape and secure with soldering tacks at the top and bottom corners of each panel.
3. Attach the vase cap and solder inside joints. (You don't need to solder the exterior seams.)

Finish:
1. Cement the panel, following the instructions in the "Crafting with Lead Came" section.
2. Clean with soap and water.
3. Paint the joints with a paint pen to hide the silvery solder. ❀

*Enlarge to 226%
for actual size*

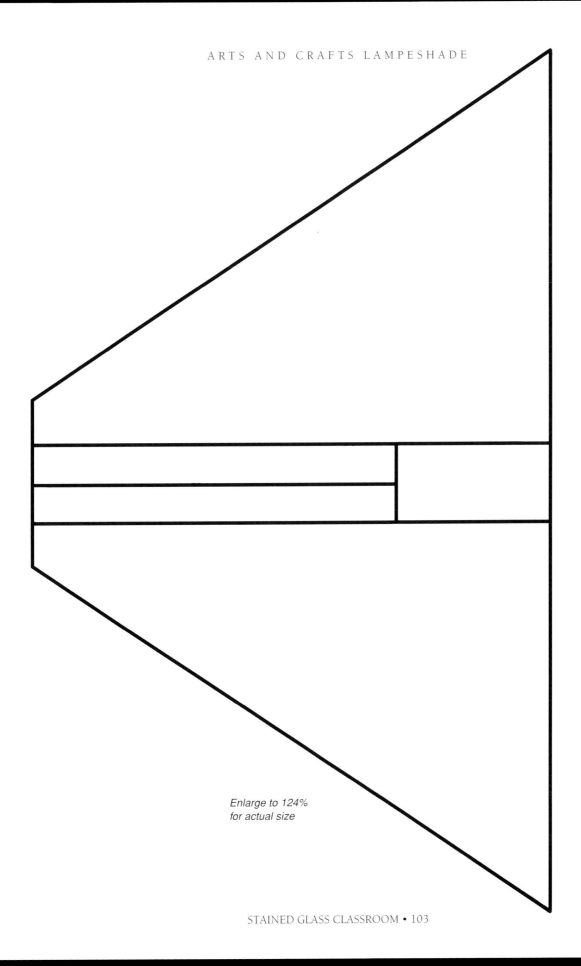

*Enlarge to 124%
for actual size*

Geometric Panel

Size: 9-1/4" x 13-1/2"
Pattern on page 108

Supplies

Glass:
Amber opalescent glass, 1 sq. ft. (for the background)
Green opalescent, 1/2 sq. ft.
Red opalescent, 4 sq. in.

Metals:
1 6-ft. strip of 3/8" flat H lead came
1 6-ft. strip of 3/16" H lead came

Tools & Other Supplies:
Cementing supplies
Black patina
Basic Tools & Supplies for Lead Came Method

Step-by-Step

Prepare & Cut Glass:
1. Make two copies of the pattern. Number and mark the grain line on each piece. Using pattern shears, cut out the design from one copy.
2. Adhere pattern pieces to the glass. Cut out each piece.
3. Use grozing pliers to remove any chips or protrusions on the glass pieces. Smooth the edges with a grinder or carborundum stone as needed to fit the pattern.

Lead Up & Solder:
1. On your work board, tape or pin the second copy of the pattern. Place the two 3/8" H lead along the edges of the work board.
2. Lead up the panel, working from one corner, placing a piece of lead, a piece of glass, and so on, until all pieces are in place. Use the grinder to smooth edges of the glass and make any necessary adjustments to keep your glass pieces within the pattern lines. Each piece must fit the pattern lines or your panel will be impossible to complete.
3. Cap off the project with the last two pieces of 3/8" lead came.
4. Solder the lead joints on the front of the panel.
5. Turn over the panel and solder the back side.

Finish:
1. Cement the panel, following the instructions in the "Crafting with Lead Came" section.
2. Clean the panel. ❀

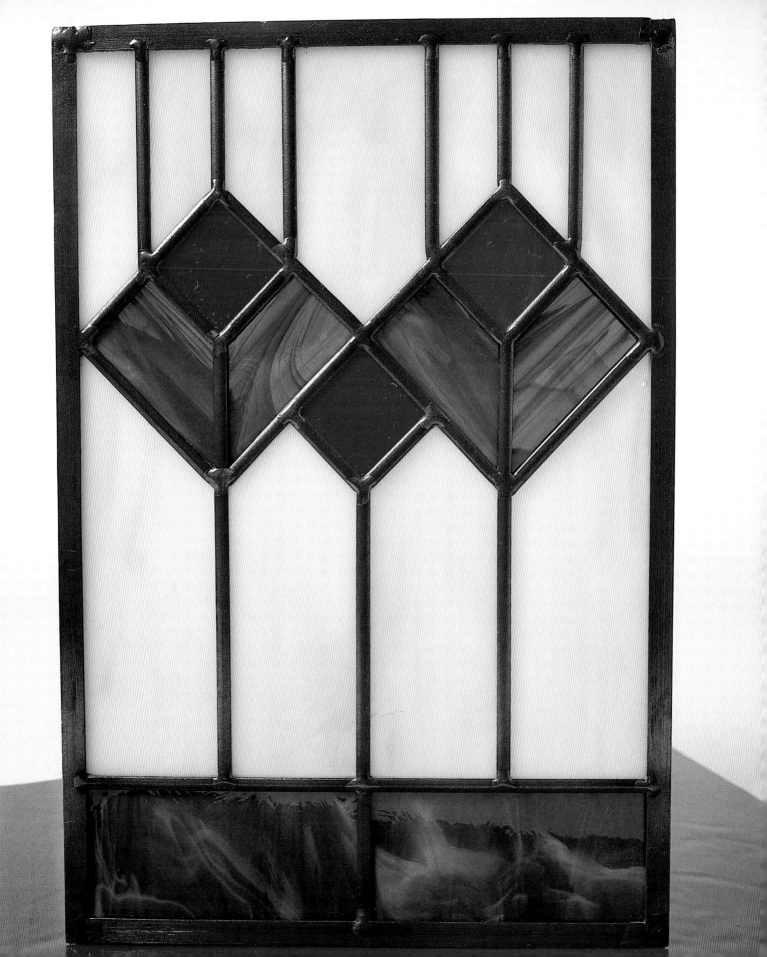

Logan's Window

My children grew up in a house filled with beveled and colored glass windows. When my daughter Sloan presented me with a beautiful little granddaughter, Logan, I wanted to create a window for her that would have special meaning for all three of us. Being the glass saver I am, I designed a window for Logan that included scraps of glass from the windows in our family home. Now, whenever Sloan and I share this window with Logan we are also sharing great family memories. Perhaps you have a favorite image or color from your childhood that you would like to share with your child or grandchild.

Since beveled glass now comes in stock sizes, it is a good idea to visit your local glass shop and see sizes of bevels they have. Then, design your panel to fit the sizes of the bevels.

Size: 24-1/2" x 14"
Pattern on page 109

Supplies

Glass:
Bevels
Clear seedy glass, 2 sq. ft. (for background)
Leaf green glass, 1 sq. ft.
Patterned glass, 2 sq. ft. (for center and border)
Rose-colored glass, 1/2 sq. ft. (for flower and corners)

Metals:
2 6-ft. strips of 3/16" H lead came
2 6-ft. strips of 1/8" H lead came
1 6-ft. strip of 1/2" U zinc came

Tools & Other Supplies:
Black patina
Cementing supplies
Basic Tools & Supplies for Lead Came Method

Step-by-Step

Prepare & Cut Glass:
1. Make two copies of the pattern. Number and mark the grain line on each piece. Using pattern shears, cut out the design from one copy.
2. Adhere pattern pieces to the glass and cut out each piece.
3. Use grozing pliers to remove any chips or protrusions on the glass pieces. Smooth the edges with a grinder or carborundum stone as needed to fit the pattern.

Lead Up & Solder:
1. On your work board, tape or pin the second copy of the pattern. Cut and place the two 3/8" H lead came pieces along the edges of the work board.
2. Lead up the panel, working from one corner, placing a piece of lead, a piece of glass, and so on, until all pieces are in place. Use the grinder to smooth edges of the glass and make any necessary adjustments to keep your glass pieces within the pattern lines. Each piece must fit the pattern lines or your panel will be impossible to complete.
3. Cap off the project with the last two pieces of 3/8" H lead came.
4. Solder the lead joints on the front of the panel.
5. Turn over the panel and solder the back side.

Finish:
1. Cement the panel, following the instructions in the "Crafting with Lead Came" section.
2. Clean the panel. ✹

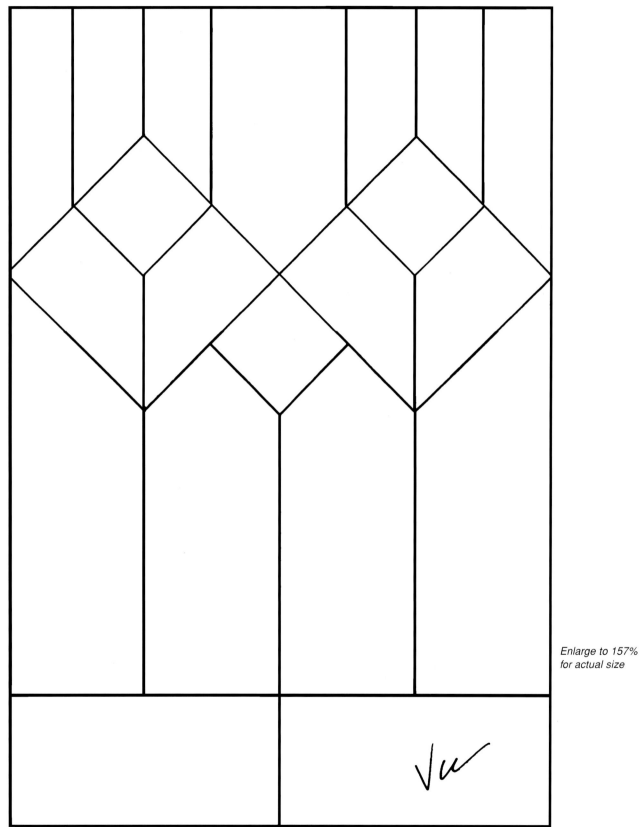

*Enlarge to 157%
for actual size*

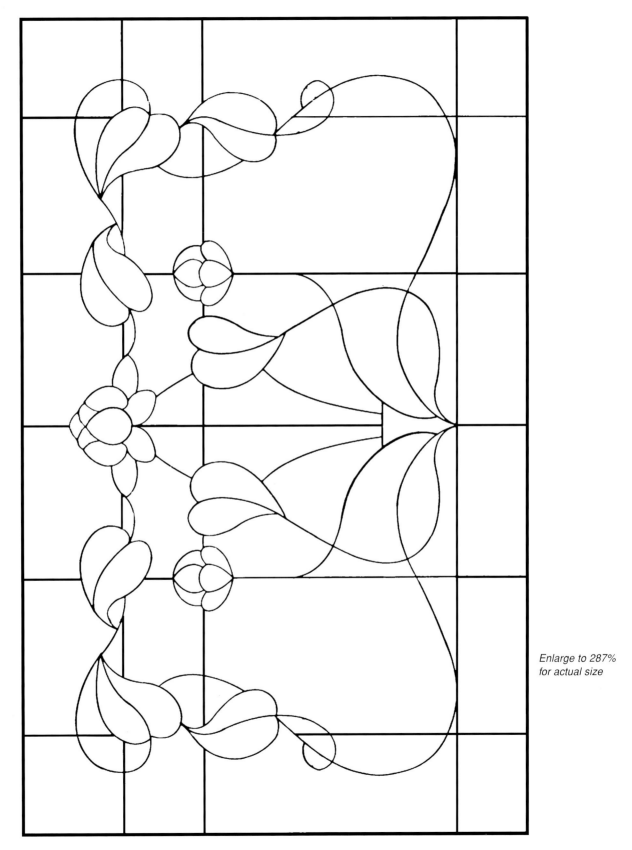

*Enlarge to 287%
for actual size*

Stained Glass Mosaics

Mosaics may look complicated, but mosaic techniques are easy to learn and many mosaic projects are quick and simple to do. Although the most common mosaic material today is tile, many early mosaics were made of glass. The mosaic projects in this book are created by cutting design motifs from glass using the patterns provided. The cut-out motifs are glued on a surface and the areas around the motifs are filled in with randomly placed small pieces of glass. The piece is then grouted—an easy process.

Making a mosaic is a great way to use small scraps of glass left over from other projects. No soldering is required.

Basic Tools & Supplies for Mosaic Method

To create glass mosaics, you need these basic tools and supplies:

- **Opalescent glass**, the same type of art glass used for many of the other projects in this book.
- **A surface** to use as a base, such as wood or terra cotta.
- **An adhesive**, such as white craft glue or silicone adhesive, to hold the glass to the surface.
- **Sanded grout**, to fill the spaces between the pieces of glass, to create a smooth surface, and to add strength and durability.
- **Grout sealer**, to seal the grout and protect it.
- **Tools**, including the same glass cutting tools you've used for other projects in this book, plus **glass nippers** (sometimes called "mosaic cutters") for breaking the small background pieces, some **craft sticks** for applying the adhesive, a **putty knife or spatula or stiff-bristled brush** for applying grout, a **sponge** for wiping grout, and some **soft cloth rags** for polishing.
- **Safety gear**, such as a dust mask and rubber gloves for working with grout, plus safety glasses for cutting glass.

Glass nippers are used to break the pieces that form the backgrounds of mosaic designs.

Crafting Glass Mosaics

Step 1 • Prepare the Pattern

1. Trace the pattern to tracing paper and transfer the design using transfer paper to white pattern paper. Make two copies. Cut out the pattern pieces to make templates.

2. Position the templates on the glass and trace around them with a felt tip marker.

Step 2 • Cut the Pieces

1. Move the glass cutter along the pattern lines drawn on the glass.

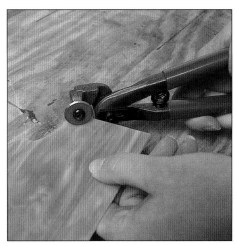

2. For the blue background pieces, use the glass nippers to break off pieces in a variety of shapes.

Step 3 • Glue Glass Pieces

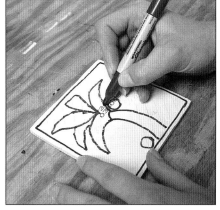

1. Use the second pattern to transfer the design to your surface. With a felt tip marker, darken the transferred lines of the pattern.

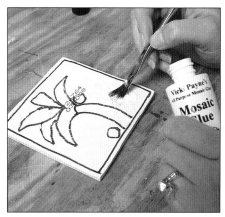

2. Apply glue to the surface, working one section at a time so the glue does not dry out before you have placed the glass pieces.

3. Place cut glass pieces on the glue. Continue to apply glue and place glass, working one area at a time. Allow 1/16" to 1/8" between glass pieces for grout.

4. When all the glass pieces are placed, let dry completely.

Step 4 • Grout

1. Mix grout according to manufacturer's instructions. Use a craft stick (shown here), a stiff-bristle brush, a putty knife or a spatula to apply the grout, pressing it into the spaces between the glass pieces. **Don't** use your fingers—the edges of the glass pieces may be sharp. It's a good idea when working with grout to wear rubber, latex, or vinyl gloves—grout is very drying to the skin.

2. When grouting is complete, fill a bowl with water, dampen a sponge, and squeeze out excess water. Wipe the mosaic to remove excess grout from the surface of the glass pieces. Rinse the sponge and wipe again. Repeat until you can see all the pieces though the grout and the grout is smooth and even with the surface of the glass. Let dry.

3. As the grout dries, a haze will form over the glass. Polish off the haze by rubbing with a soft cloth rag until the glass gleams.

Nuggets

Nuggets

If you wish to use this pattern to make coasters, cut circles from glass rather than using nuggets so your coasters will be flat.

Palm Tree Coaster pattern – actual size

Palm Tree Coasters or Tiles

Standard 4" x 4" white ceramic tiles, available at tile and home improvement stores, are used as the base for this design.

Supplies

For two coasters
Glass:
Green, 4" square
Sky blue opalescent, 4" square
Scraps of brown glass
4 amber glass nuggets

Tools & Other Supplies:
2 white ceramic tiles, 4" square
Basic Tools & Supplies for Mosaic Method

Follow instructions on pages 111 and 112 for making tiles.

Acorn Serving Tray

Fall is the time for friends, parties, and long Sunday dinners. This little wooden and mosaic glass tray is just as welcoming as it is useful. I purchased a new unfinished wooden tray as a base, but you might be lucky and find an old one from the 50s.

A project like this really shows the beauty of opalescent glass—the rich green of the oak leaves and the warmth of the soft opalescent background. Cutting the glass into tiny rectangles and placing them like rows of bricks provides a less cluttered background than that of some mosaics.

Size: 9" x 12"

Supplies

Glass:
Caramel opalescent, 1 sq. ft. (background)
Green opalescent, 1/2 sq. ft. (leaves)
Olive opalescent, 1/2 sq. ft. (leaves)
Brown opalescent, 1/4 sq. ft. (acorn)

Tools & Other Supplies:
Wooden serving tray
Oak wood stain, waterbase
Acrylic craft paint - Basil green
Sandpaper
Transfer paper, tracing paper, and pencil
Ruler
Clear wood sealer
Basic Tools & Supplies for Mosaic Method

Step-by-Step

Prepare:

1. Sand the finish of the tray to provide a smooth surface for gluing the mosaic pieces. *Option:* If your tray is covered in layers of paint, you may wish to strip the paint.
2. Paint the outside and the bottom of the tray with basic green craft paint. Let dry. Sand very lightly with fine sandpaper. Wipe away dust.
3. Apply a coat of stain to the inside edges of the tray and the green-painted exterior. Keep design area as clean as possible. Allow tray to dry completely.
4. Apply wood sealer to tray surface.
5. Trace the pattern and enlarge to fit your tray. Make an extra copy of the leaf and acorn patterns to cut up for templates.
6. Use transfer paper and a pencil to transfer the design to the surface.
7. Use a ruler to draw 1/2" rows across the background. This will help keep your mosaic "bricks" straight.

Cut the Glass:

1. Cut the caramel background glass into 1/4" strips, using a ruler or a strip cutter to help you make straight cuts. *TIP:* It is easier to cut narrow pieces into short (6") strips. Cut the strips into bricks.
2. Glue the templates onto the green and brown glass using rubber cement or spray adhesive.

3. Use your glass cutter to cut out the shapes. Use your grozing pliers to help you shape the pieces as you work. *Option:* Cut the glass into small pieces and fill in the shapes, using grozing pliers to shape the pieces.

Glue:

1. Glue the acorns, stem, and leaves to the surface of the tray, applying a coat of glue to the area and positioning the pieces. Allow a small, even amount of space between each piece for grout.
2. Glue the background pieces. It's best to work from left to right, gluing one complete row at a time. Be sure to stagger the bricks on consecutive rows. Use your grozing pliers or nippers to trim the background pieces around the design so you can completely cover the surface with glass. Allow the glue to dry completely (overnight).

Grout & Finish:

1. Mix the grout according to the manufacturer's instructions and tint to match your background glass. I mixed a small amount of waterbase "oak" stain with white grout to achieve a warm, rich vanilla color. (You can use most waterbase and acrylic paints to tint white grout.)
2. Apply grout, wipe away excess, and let dry.
3. Polish the surface with a soft cloth.
4. Apply a couple of coats of grout sealer to protect the surface from coffee or wine stains. ❀

Enlarge to 161% for actual size

Grape Canisters

Mosaic "panels" are colorful additions to square glass canisters. The panels are framed with strips of brass came.

Supplies

Glass:
Yellow opalescent, 1 sq. ft.
Red opalescent, 1/2 sq. ft.
Green opalescent, 4" x 4"
8 to 24 small purple opalescent nuggets

Tools & Other Supplies:
3 clear glass canisters - small, medium, large
Transfer and tracing paper
Black grout
Masking tape
Adhesive-backed brass came
Came saw *or* hacksaw
Basic Tools & Supplies for Mosaic Method

Step-by-Step

Prepare:

1. Clean the canisters and allow to dry.
2. Trace the pattern from book onto tracing paper. Adjust as needed to fit canisters. Make one copy of pattern for each canister plus an extra one to use as a template.
3. Cut the canister patterns so they will fit inside the canisters. Tape in place inside canisters with design facing out.
4. On the outside, tape off the design area.

Cut & Glue:

1. Cut out the leaf from the template pattern. Place the leaf template on the green glass and trace around it with a marker. Trace as many leaves as needed.
2. Use your glass cutter to cut out the leaf shapes. *Option:* Cut the glass into small pieces with nippers and fill in the shapes of the elements. Use your grozing pliers to help you shape the pieces as you go.
3. Glue leaves and nuggets to the surface of the canisters, using the patterns as guides. Work one canister at a time, applying a coat of glue to the area and positioning the pieces. Allow a small, even amount of space between each piece for grout.
4. Use your grozing pliers or nippers to trim the background pieces around the design. Working one area at a time, glue the background pieces, covering the surface completely with glass. Allow the glue to dry completely. Use the photo as a guide.

Grout & Finish:

1. Mix grout according to manufacturer's instructions.
2. Use a spatula or putty knife to apply the grout, pressing it into the spaces between the glass pieces.
3. Fill a bowl with water. Dampen a sponge and squeeze out excess water. Wipe the piece to remove excess grout from the surface. Rinse the sponge and wipe again. Repeat until you can see all the pieces through the grout and the grout is smooth and even with the surface. Let dry.
4. As the grout dries, a haze will form over the glass. Polish off the haze by rubbing with a soft cloth rag until the glass pieces gleam.

5. Allow the grout to dry completely. Remove the tape. Apply a couple of coats of grout sealer to protect the surface.
6. Cut the adhesive-backed brass came to frame the designs, using a came saw or hacksaw. Attach the came around the mosaic designs. ✽

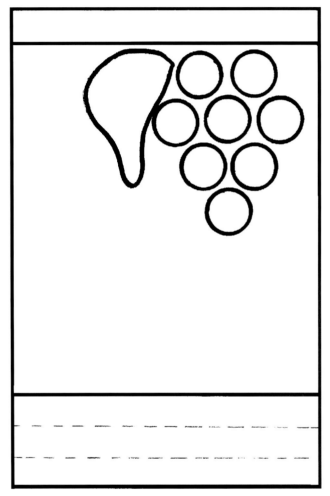

Pattern is actual size

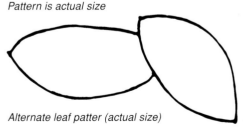

Alternate leaf patter (actual size)

Instructions on page 120

Enlarge to 153% for actual size

Palm Tree Table

A wood base makes a great surface for stained glass mosaics. You can enlarge this pattern to fit your outdoor picnic table or keep it small and simple. In the smaller size (as it here), it's perfect for a snack table on the patio or a bedside stand for the phone and clock. Use bright colors and have fun with this sea and sand motif.

Size: 12" round

Supplies

Glass:

Dark blue opalescent, 1 sq. ft. (for background)

White opalescent, 1/2 sq. ft.

Brown opalescent, 6" square

Green opalescent, 8" square

48 medium yellow opaque glass nuggets

Tools & Other Supplies:

12" wood round *or* wood sized to fit tabletop

Transfer paper, tracing paper, and pencil

Acrylic craft paint - Deep pink

Clear wood sealer

Basic Tools & Supplies for Mosaic Method

Step-by-Step

Prepare:

1. Paint the exposed tabletop or wood round with pink craft paint. Keep design area as clean as possible. Allow to dry completely.
2. Apply wood sealer to painted area. Let dry.
3. Trace the design and transfer to the surface. Make an extra copy of the palm tree pattern to cut up for templates.
4. Glue the templates to the green and brown glass using rubber cement or spray adhesive.

Cut & Glue:

1. Use your glass cutter to cut out the shapes. *Option:* Cut the glass into small mosaic pieces and fill in the shapes of the design. Use your grozing pliers to help you shape the pieces as you go.
2. Glue the tree trunk and palm fronds to the tabletop, applying a coat of glue to the area and positioning the pieces. Allow a small, even amount of space between each piece for grout.
3. Glue the background pieces. Use your grozing pliers or nippers to trim the background pieces around the design, covering the surface completely with glass. Allow the glue to dry overnight—it should be completely dry.

Grout & Finish:

1. Mix grout according to manufacturer's instructions. Use a spatula or putty knife to apply the grout, pressing it into the spaces between the nuggets.
2. Fill a bowl with water. Dampen a sponge and squeeze out excess water. Wipe the piece to remove excess grout from the surfaces of the glass. Rinse the sponge and wipe again. Repeat until you can see all the pieces through the grout and the grout is smooth and even between the pieces and tapered down to the tabletop between the nuggets that form the border. Let dry.
3. As the grout dries, a haze will form over the glass. Polish off the haze by rubbing with a soft cloth rag until the glass gleams.
4. Apply a couple of coats of grout sealer to protect the surface. ✽

Sunflower Shade

My laundry room ceiling light fixture was really bland, and the answer was this easy-to-create mosaic lampshade. Working with the existing glass shade, I created this sunny sunflower design. I like working with the white grout because it doesn't distract from the design or reduce the usable light that comes through the shade.

Look up! Any light source is a possible opportunity for art glass—perhaps one of your ceiling fixtures could use an art glass makeover.

Size: 8" round

Supplies

Glass:

White opalescent, 1 sq. ft. (for background)
Yellow opalescent, 8" square
Light yellow opalescent, 4" square
Light green opalescent, 4" square
Light brown opalescent, 4" square

Tools & Other Supplies:

8" glass ceiling dome light fixture cover
White grout
Transfer paper, tracing paper, and pencil
Basic Tools & Supplies for Mosaic Method

Step-by-Step

Prepare:

1. Clean dome thoroughly with soap and water and let dry.
2. Trace the pattern and transfer to the surface. Make an extra copy of the pattern and cut out the pieces for templates.
3. Adhere the cutouts to the glass, using rubber cement or spray adhesive.

Cut & Glue:

1. Use your glass nippers to cut out the shapes. Use your grozing pliers to help shape the pieces as you go.
2. Working one area at a time, apply a coat of glue to the area and position the pieces following the pattern. Allow a small, even amount of space between each piece for grout. Allow the glue to dry overnight—it should be completely dry.

Grout & Finish:

1. Mix grout according to manufacturer's instructions. Use a spatula or putty knife to apply the grout, pressing it into the spaces between the nuggets.
2. Fill a bowl with water. Dampen a sponge and squeeze out excess water. Wipe the piece to remove excess grout from the surfaces of the glass. Rinse the sponge and wipe again. Repeat until you can see all the pieces through the grout and the grout is smooth and even between the pieces. Let dry.
3. As the grout dries, a haze will form over the glass. Polish off the haze by rubbing with a soft cloth rag until the glass gleams.
4. Apply a couple of coats of grout sealer to protect the surface. ✿

Pattern is actual size

Glass Nugget Balls

A simple mosaic of glass nuggets makes a colorful decorative accent. A plastic foam ball is the base.

Supplies

Glass:
Glass nuggets - at least 48, in the color of your choice

Tools & Other Supplies:
3" round plastic foam ball
Basic Tools & Supplies For Mosaic Projects

Step-by-Step

1. Apply glue to the backs of the nuggets and place on the surface of the foam ball. Allow to thoroughly dry.
2. Mix grout according to manufacturer's instructions. Use a spatula or putty knife to apply the grout, pressing it into the spaces between the nuggets.
3. Fill a bowl with water. Dampen a sponge and squeeze out excess water. Wipe the piece to remove excess grout from the surfaces of the nuggets. Rinse the sponge and wipe again. Repeat until you can see all the pieces through the grout and the grout is smooth and even with the surface. Let dry.
4. As the grout dries, a haze will form over the nuggets. Polish off the haze by rubbing with a soft cloth rag until the nuggets gleam. ❁

Dish Wind Chime

This BONUS PROJECT is an easy project that requires very little tools.
It shows just how fun and versatile working with glass can be.

Supplies

Glass:
Antique glass dish
Cathedral glass, 1/2 sq. ft.

Tools & Other Supplies:
Clear monofilament fishing line
Decorative glass beads
12 gauge copper wire
Drill and drill bit

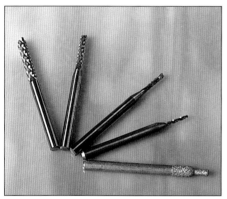

Drill bits for glass.

Drilling holes in the glass dish. Using a lined box for drilling cushions the glass and contains the drilling dust. Be sure to wear a dust mask and eye protection when drilling glass.

Step-by-Step

1. Drill one hole at the top of the dish. Drill three evenly spaced holes along the bottom edge. As a precaution, line a plastic container with foam padding. Fill container half-full of water. Place glass to be drilled under water and drill hole. The water cools the glass and prevents breakage.
2. Cut three cathedral glass strips, each 1" x 12-1/2". Drill a hole at the top of each strip.
3. Cut four pieces of copper wire, each approximately 12" long. This can be adjusted.
4. Arrange beads on the four wires. Attach one wire at the top of the dish for hanging and secure on other side of the hole with a bead.
5. Attach remaining three wires to the bottom of the dish by inserting in holes. Twist the ends of the wire to secure in place.
6. Attach a glass strip to each wire, securing the ends.
7. Use monofilament fishing line for hanging. ✸

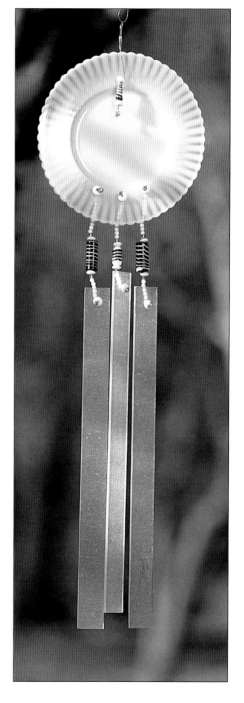

Metric Conversion Chart

Inches to Millimeters and Centimeters

Inches	MM	CM	Inches	MM	CM
1/8	3	.3	2	51	5.1
1/4	6	.6	3	76	7.6
3/8	10	1.0	4	102	10.2
1/2	13	1.3	5	127	12.7
5/8	16	1.6	6	152	15.2
3/4	19	1.9	7	178	17.8
7/8	22	2.2	8	203	20.3
1	25	2.5	9	229	22.9
1-1/4	32	3.2	10	254	25.4
1-1/2	38	3.8	11	279	27.9
1-3/4	44	4.4	12	305	30.5

Yards to Meters

Yards	Meters	Yards	Meters
1/8	.11	3	2.74
1/4	.23	4	3.66
3/8	.34	5	4.57
1/2	.46	6	5.49
5/8	.57	7	6.40
3/4	.69	8	7.32
7/8	.80	9	8.23
1	.91	10	9.14
2	1.83		

Index